D1624342

OPERA

A CRASH
COURSE

OPERA

A CRASH COURSE

STEPHEN PETTITT

WATSON-GUPTILL
PUBLICATIONS
New York

Copyright © THE IVY PRESS LIMITED 1998

First published in the United States in 1998 by
Watson-Guptill Publications, a division of BPI
Communications, Inc., 1515 Broadway, New York,
NY 10036

All rights reserved. No part of this book may
be reproduced or used in any form or by any
means – graphic, electronic, or mechanical, including
photocopying, recording, taping, or information
storage and retrieval systems – without written
permission of the publisher.

Library of Congress Catalog Card Number: 97-62554

ISBN 0-8230-0975-0

This book was conceived, designed, and produced by
THE IVY PRESS LIMITED
2/3 St Andrews Place
Lewes, East Sussex, BN7 1UP

Art director: PETER BRIDGEWATER
Designer: JANE LANAWAY
Commissioning Editor: VIV CROOT
Managing Editor: ANNE TOWNLEY
Page layout: CHRIS LANAWAY
Picture research: VANESSA FLETCHER
Illustrations: CURTIS TAPPENDEN *and* ANDREW ROBERTS

Printed and bound in Hong Kong

1 2 3 4 5 6 7 8 9 10/06 05 04 03 02 01 00 99 98

DEDICATION

*In honor of my mother
and her courage,
and with love to Harry Cheung.*

Contents

Introduction

ABOVE What's the story: surtitles translate as you listen.

Why write this guide to opera? First, to express a complex history as clearly as possible. Second, to show just how diverse opera is. La Bohème *or* Aida *are powerful and enduring works, but also out there are hundreds – even thousands – of operas that never get performed at all. Not because they're bad, but because opera houses have to stay solvent and dare not risk too many empty seats. There is a mission to support neglected operas – both the old and, more importantly, the new, without which opera as an art form will stagnate into simply another money-making commodity (like, dare I say it, the musical – about which you will find little in this book; and operetta is another story altogether).*

Dating Operas

The convention for assigning a date to an opera is to give the date of first performance – for older operas, that's often the only date of which one can be certain, anyway – so, unless otherwise indicated, that is the practice followed here.

" ☆ "

Star Boxes

Starred Boxes contain gosh facts; you didn't need to know them, but they beef up your music cred. Just the thing for pompous dinner parties.

How This Course Works

This course proceeds more or less chronologically, although each double-page spread is dedicated to one composer, a group, or connected works. And on each spread there are regular features. It won't take you long to work them out.

So the message of Opera: A Crash Course *is not to take what you are offered, but to study the wine list carefully, and perhaps select that impertinent little number from seventeenth-century Naples, or that intriguing-looking offering from 1970s' Europe.*

One word of warning. Don't expect opera simply – or always – to entertain you. Opera, like all art, should provide a way into the human spirit. If a work seems difficult and long, try your damnedest not to walk out. Tell yourself that someone out there – the composer – has agonized long and hard about how to say something. Try to enter this world, a world that is also an important corner of yours.

Names of Note *widens the scope, providing name-checks in a selective list of other composers and performers influenced by, contemporary with or connected to the main man (or, rarely, woman); you may not always get musicians. Sometimes the names of patrons are just as illuminating. Plus, you get to show off more.*

Timeline

Not so much a timeline, because it's impossible to run a continuous chronology: composers are constantly tripping over each others' batons, so more of a contextual commentary, a selected list of major events happening at the time the composers in question were living, to demonstrate how all aspects of life are, inevitably, fogbound in the same *Zeitgeist*. It's also a bit brainboggling to discover that the telephone and *Carmen* are contemporary.

STEPHEN PETTITT

LEFT *Mathis der Maler*, old story, new blood.

4000–3500 B.C. Harps and flutes are played in Ancient Egypt, the former probably developed from the archer's bow.

776 B.C. At the first recorded Olympic Games, featuring horse racing, boxing, wrestling, running and pentathlon, women are not even admitted as spectators.

390 In the Christian Church, the first psalms are sung, as responses by two choirs, or by a priest and congregation singing alternate verses.

1500~1580
The Birth of Opera
A Pure Music Drama

Usually, when it comes to classical forms in music, nobody can say that the symphony, concerto, or sonata was invented at such and such a time, in such and such a place, by such and such people. Those musical forms just came about – a few innovative radicals were behind them, of course, but in general they simply evolved. (And, like all things that evolve, they never assumed static shapes, convenient though that would be for those who like everything – even something as freely expressive as music – to fit neatly into little boxes.) Opera, however, is slightly different; opera, you see, was invented (sort of).

ABOVE Costume design for Monteverdi's *Poppea*.

O nce upon a time, a group of Florentine intellectual-cum-literary radicals, whom we know collectively as the Camerata, sat around at one of their regular meetings dominated by two leading figures, *Vincenzo GALILEI* (*c.*1520–91) and *Giovanni BARDI* (1534–1612), discussing, as usual, the Meaning of Art, Life, the Universe, and Everything, and came up with the idea of opera. Well, it wasn't quite as simple as that.

What this gathering was actually aiming to do was recreate the ideals and principles of ancient Greek drama. An ancient Greek plot was a good start. And the sources they had on hand – contemporaneous reports, rather than the first-hand evidence of original manuscripts – suggested that Greek drama was either sung or declaimed in such a way as to heighten (yet maintain the clarity of) the texts. So they decided that their new works

A True Revolutionary

Jacopo Peri may not go down in history as one of the greatest composers of all time, but he was certainly one of music's true revolutionaries. His first opera – and the first opera of all time – *Dafne*, premiered in 1597, is now lost. But his second, *Euridice*, composed in 1600 for the Medicis, survives. Written less than a decade before Monteverdi's first effort (see p.12), *Euridice* cannot musically hold a candle to the master, but if you ever get a chance to see it, don't pass it up. This is where opera began.

750 In France and Germany, beds become popular, while in Bavaria hops are used for the first time as beer wort.

1075–1100 French troubadours, setting poetry to the music of their own harp accompaniment, raise the profile of secular music.

1348–52 The Black Death, an epidemic of bubonic plague caused by the fleas on migrating Asian black rats, kills up to half of Europe's population.

ABOVE Berg's *Lulu*, based on the Pandora myth.

should likewise follow the contours of dramatic declamation, with embellishments on particularly meaningful words.

All of this was mere theory, of course, until someone put up his hand and declared that he would have a go at writing something resembling what the group envisaged. This daredevil was *Jacopo PERI* (1561–1633).

SPECTACLE OR SUBTLETY?

All right, it wasn't quite as sudden as that – and to be honest, Peri wasn't the only one to have a go at this new-fangled *dramma per musica* (it was the English who started calling it opera, meaning literally "works,"

much later in the seventeenth century). Other composers were Peri's rival singers *Emilio DE' CAVALIERI* (*c.*1550–1602), whose *La rappresentazione di Anima e di Corpo* (1600) is often cited as the first oratorio, and *Giulio CACCINI* (*c.*1548–1618). And music drama as an idea had been around since at least medieval times, when liturgical dramas and mystery plays were commonplace. In the sixteenth century, the pastoral play and the courtly *intermedio*, seen between the acts of spoken plays, held sway. The Medicis – wouldn't you know it – were well known for their lavish *intermedii*, sycophantically allegorical episodes designed to flaunt their riches and adorn ceremonies. But when a purer music drama – opera – came along, the scene was set for opera's longest-standing argument, between those who prize its spectacle and those who value its more subtle potential. The rest is history.

RIGHT Cherubini's *Médée*, based on the story of Medea, the Witch Queen.

1580 The English *Greensleeves* folk tune gets its first mention in the Stationers' Company Register, where it is called "a new Northern dittye."

1589 The fork makes its first appearance at the French court. Table manners begin.

1596 Water closets are installed in England at the Queen's Palace, Richmond – a triumph of design by Sir John Harington.

1580~1610
The Full Monte
Monteverdi, Gods, and Humans

ABOVE Monteverdi, father of opera.

Now that we know the basic reason for opera's invention, it's time for an admission. Those first operas were all very interesting, but not great music. Anybody who knows anything agrees that the first opera to achieve the status of greatness was L'Orfeo, *by the Cremona-born composer Claudio MONTEVERDI (1567–1643). He wrote* L'Orfeo – *literally* The Orpheus – *for the carnival season in 1607 at the court of the Gonzagas at Mantua, where he was employed. He'd already made his mark with his radically bold harmonies and expressive text setting.*

Like him, the Gonzagas were progressive. So was Monteverdi's opera. By all accounts it was a smashing success. Monteverdi was enough of his own man to change librettist *Alessandro STRIGGIO's* (*c.*1573–1630) ending, which originally had our hero Orfeo being dismembered by the frenzied Maenads, as per Ovid. Much better to send the audience home happy. So instead, down comes a god on a cloud – the *deus ex machina* that became a standard feature of baroque opera – to rescue Orfeo from hell's torment.

ORPHEUS

This guy features in the world's first opera, as well as in superb works by Rossi (1647), Sartorio (1672), and Gluck (1762, revised 1774), and he stars in Offenbach's Parisian operetta and in Birtwistle's 1980s' masterpiece. Why? Well, Orpheus, son of Apollo, is the mythical Greek poet and minstrel, the man who proves that music has the power to melt the hardest of hearts. He's a great ad for the art.

1600 The continuo group becomes an important part of the musical scene, often including lutes, harps, and strings.

1604 In London, the Worshipful Company of Musicians receives its royal charter.

1606 In Rome, the first open-air opera takes place. It starts a trend for occasional *al fresco* performances staged in classical arenas or natural amphitheaters.

LOVE AND DEATH

The reason *Orfeo* works so well is that Monteverdi clothes Greek mythology – Orpheus being the minstrel son of Apollo, who marries, then loses, Eurydice – in the conventions of sixteenth-century drama, mixes new and old musical styles, and colors his music in vivid hues.

He also wrote out in full a series of extravagant ornamentations for Orfeo's great set-piece, pleading for entry into Hades, "Possente spirto." Plus, it's a work about the trials of love and death, emotions that every human knows.

TO NOTE / NAMES

Besides Monteverdi and the early triumvirate of Peri, Caccini, and Cavalieri (see pp.10–11), you might like to look up **Stefano Landi** *(c.1586–1639), composer of the first Roman secular opera (La morte d'Orfeo), and* **Michelangelo** *(1602–56) and* **Luigi** *(1598–1653)* **Rossi.** *And there are many other, more obscure composers – Loreto Vittori, Filippo Vitali, who are they? Just as significant as the major composers are the librettists –* **Alessandro Striggio** *(c.1573–1630), author of the text for Monteverdi's Orfeo, was one of the best – but one thing at a time.*

Monteverdi's operatic career continued the next year with *L'Arianna.* Apparently, it was another huge success. Unfortunately, we can judge it today solely on the merits of "Arianna's Lament," the only part of the opera that has survived. In the intervening year, Monteverdi's wife had died and it's tempting to attribute the depth of feeling in the lament to that sad experience.

Who Were the Gonzagas?

You mean you don't know? Only one of Italy's most important ruling dynasties, who governed the state (and city) of Mantua from the early fourteenth until the early eighteenth century. They also happened to employ Monteverdi, as well as a number of other highly distinguished composers. There were good composers in the family, too. Generally good eggs, musically speaking.

LEFT Orpheus (at the harp) keeps a wary eye out for monsters as he plays to Pluto and Persephone in the Underworld (Brueghel the Elder, 1568–1625).

1608 The first checks, or "cash letters" come into use in The Netherlands, revolutionizing the carrying of money.

1632 Monteverdi takes holy orders, possibly catalyzed by losing 12 operas for Marma and Mantua in the sack of Mantua and by the ensuing plague.

1635 The speed of hackney coaches is restricted to 3 mph in London.

1610~1650

The First Great Opera

Monte's *Poppea*

ABOVE Homer's hero Ulysses (star of M.'s opera, *Ulisse*) squares up to the sturdy beggar Irus.

After Venice opened its theaters to the public in the 1630s, Monteverdi – since 1613 Master of Music of the Venetian Republic and music boss at St. Mark's Basilica – composed three new operas, Il ritorno d'Ulisse in patria (1641), Le nozze d'Enea con Lavinia (again lost), and L'incoronazione di Poppea (1642). The surviving works both show a new interest in deeper aspects of human psychology, and incorporate a huge variety of human types. Dialogue and comic relief now become part of opera's stock-in-trade.

Ulisse, whose brilliant text was by Giacomo BADOARO (1602–54), turns Homer's mythological characters into recognizable human beings, in the process working inexorably toward its happy climax. In *Poppea*, the libretto by *Giovanni Francesco* BUSENELLO (1598–1659) is based on historical fact, elevating to heroic status one of the most evil rulers in the history of the world, the Emperor Nero. His intended, Poppea, isn't exactly a pleasant character, either. But miraculously Monteverdi gets us to sympathize with this motley crew of highly flawed beings. It's an opera about conflicting morality and love.

RIGHT Janet Baker sings *Poppea* at Sadler's Wells, a London theater.

Early Venetian Theaters

Venice, as eager as ever to be different, was nearly the first city to have an opera theater for the paying public – the Teatro S. Cassiano (which Francesco Cavalli later graced), which saw its first production (Francesco Manelli's since forgotten *Andromeda*) in 1637. But though Padua beat Venice by a short neck, it was in the Serene City that public opera flourished. In 1639 the Teatro di SS. Giovanni e Paolo (with which Monteverdi was associated) opened for opera; in 1640 the Teatro S. Moïse followed; and in 1641 the Teatro Novissimo. Later in the century two more theaters, the Teatro Sant'Apollinare and the Teatro Vendramin, staged extended seasons. All these institutions were privately owned, commercial enterprises, vying with each other for the best stage machinery and the most eminent composers. The famous and beautiful Teatro La Fenice, which was recently razed to the ground under suspicious circumstances, was not built until 1792.

1637 The commercial Dutch tulip trade undergoes a collapse. People send lilies.

1641 Arsenic is prescribed medicinally for the first time, although Mithridates of Pontus (c.100 B.C.) is said to have protected himself against poisoning by taking regular small doses.

1644 Antonio Stradivari(us) is born in Italy. The greatest violin-maker of all time, his fame will spread and his violins command extravagant prices.

Ghost Writers

Here's the bombshell – Monteverdi didn't actually write all the notes in these masterpieces himself. Both text and music of the famous final love duet in *Poppea*, for instance, are probably by one Benedetto Ferrari – a useful fact to let drop casually at the bar.

A HELPING HAND

Opera at this time was a flexible form, subject to all sorts of alterations, additions, and excisions, according to the circumstances of its performances. It was also the product of the same workshop mentality that reigned in the visual arts. Need a quick recitative? Get the young apprentice to do it!

TO NOTE **NAMES**

Poppea *paved the way for many other Italian opera composers –* **Francesco Cavalli** *(1602–76) and* **Antonio Cesti** *(1623–69, whose work includes a wonderful comedy called* Il pomo d'oro – *how could an opera called "The Tomato" not be funny?) Later came* **Antonio Lotti** *(c.1667–1740),* **Tomaso Albinoni** *(1671–1751),* **Antonio Caldara** *(c.1670–1736), and, in Naples,* **Alessandro Scarlatti** *(1660–1725). Opera became eminently exportable, in some cases acting as a catalyst for the invention of native operas, while in others suppressing the evolution of a genuinely native art.*

BELOW Homer entertains the crowds at the gates of Athens with his ripping yarn, the *Iliad* (Guillaume Lethière). Homer's tales made great libretti.

1665 In New York the first-known horse race to be run on turf takes place.

1666 Cheddar cheese make its first appearance on English tables, as the Great Fire of London ravages the capital.

1683 One Mr. Sadler discovers a well with reputed medicinal qualities in his north London garden and enlarges his buildings to accommodate and entertain visitors. Thus Sadler's Wells musical entertainment comes about.

1 6 5 0 ~ 1 7 1 0

Opera in England
Dido and Aeneas

ABOVE Henry Purcell, England's greatest composer, after a chalk drawing attributed to Godfrey Kneller (1646–1723).

Having invented the form, Italy got off to a cracking operatic start. In the mid-seventeenth century, France and Germany began to make their moves. But Britain languished behind. Even the great Henry PURCELL (1659–95) mostly composed semi-operas, plays from which lumps of text were removed to make way for lumps of incidental music and masques. Influenced by Nicholas LANIER (1588–1666), who set English words to Italian-style recitative, a composite work called The Siege of Rhodes *was written in 1656. Designed to circumvent Oliver Cromwell's ban on spoken drama, it came to nothing much and has now been lost.*

Purcell's only proper opera was *Dido and Aeneas*, until recently thought to have been written for performance at Josias Priest's boarding school for girls in Chelsea in 1689 (though why, no one quite knows). In fact it's probably earlier. It's perfect for those low on operatic stamina, because it lasts barely an hour. There are some colorful characterizations (witches and sailors, and a very hissable sorceress). As kings go, Aeneas is a bit of a wimp. But the star role of

Dido, Queen of Carthage, is one of majestic and tragic splendor. Her suicide air, "When I am laid in earth," is a moving example of a ground-bass aria.

RIGHT Sandra Browne sings *Dido*, the tragic African queen, in a production by English National Opera.

1687 "Pretty, witty Nellie" Gwyn, of oranges and "breeches parts" fame, dies after having at least one son – and possibly more – by King Charles II.

1698 In Russia a tax is imposed on all men who wear beards.

1700 In Berlin it is unmarried women who suddenly find themselves being taxed – does a rash of weddings ensue?

What's Behind the Masque?

A masque was a stage entertainment (often based on mythology) that combined poetry, singing, music, acting, and dancing. The master of the English masque was Ben Jonson (1572–1637).

LEFT *Dido and Aeneas* by Theodore van Thulden (1606–79); Dido falls in love with Aeneas, then kills herself when the gods order him to abandon her.

NAMES TO NOTE

Other alleged early operas by Englishmen include Lanier's setting (c.1617) of Ben Jonson's masque Lovers Made Men *(nice title, that) – now lost; William Congreve's* The Judgement of Paris, *which was set four times by* **John Eccles** *(c.1660–1735),* **Gottfried Finger** *(c.1660–1730), Purcell's brother* **Daniel** *(c.1660–1717), and* **Thomas Arne** *(1710–78) – Arne's Milton-inspired* Comus *(1738) and* Alfred *(1740) are more masque than opera;* **Thomas Clayton's** *opera seria* Arsinoe *(1705) and* Rosamond *(1707);* **John Eccles'** *unperformed* Semele *(1707); and* **Eccles'** *and* **Finger's** *jointly written* The Loves of Mars and Venus *(1696). But that was about the sum total as far as native-born baroque English composers were concerned.*

THE CASTRATI CURIOSITY

Dido was followed by a few well-intentioned efforts in English around the turn of the century. But a popular Italian import guaranteed their failure. The musically and otherwise fascinating castrati – male singers who in boyhood had been deprived of vital elements of their manhood – made Italian opera popular in London. In 1705 Sir John Vanbrugh opened the Haymarket (later the King's) Theatre to cope with the demand. And then one *George Frideric* HANDEL (1685–1759) blew into town.

RIGHT Vanbrugh's Haymarket Theatre, London, where all Purcell's major operas were premiered.

1651 The young King Louis XIV of France features in a court ballet as a dancer.

1664 Lully introduces the coiled brass horn as an orchestral instrument in his comedy ballet *La Princess d'Elide*, thereby giving it its current name, the "French horn."

1671 Madame de Sévigné begins writing her famous letters on life at the French court to her daughter.

1650~1700

The Gallic Muse
Lully versus Charpentier

As in England, most of the first true operas in France were Italian imports, though needless to say the French made their own minor improvements to the genre. They inserted extra ballet music and added several layers of extravagance to the staging. But these innovations didn't really catch on, and it wasn't until the 1660s and 1670s that a truly distinctive native opera finally emerged. It was a concoction of Italian opera and other musico-dramatic forms, with a large measure of influence from the rich tradition of French spoken drama – all presented with spectacle and swagger, no expense spared.

The man responsible was Italian-born Jean-Baptiste LULLY (1632–87, aka *Giovanni Battista LULLI*), a colorful character who ingratiated himself with the French royal court of the Sun King, Louis XIV, a monarch besotted with *gloire* and absolute power. Lully therefore became the first director of the Paris Opéra, or Académie Royale de Musique, as it was

Quinault

Lully's favored librettist was Philippe Quinault (1635–88). Their partnership began with relatively modest court entertainments, like the eclogue (short pastoral poem) *La grotte de Versailles* (1668). When Lully achieved success with his setting of Quinault's *Cadmus et Hermione* (1673), he gave his wordsmith a contract – one libretto a year for 4,000 livres. The result was eleven *tragédies en musique* and a pair of large-scale ballets, although the association was interrupted between 1677 and 1680 when Quinault's portrayal of Juno in *Isis* was taken to be a less than flattering reference to Louis XIV's current mistress. *Whoops alors!*

1677 In Paris, ice cream establishes a popular following as a fashionable dessert. Because of its expense, small, covered "ice cups" are created, which limit the size of the portions.

1680 The famous flightless dodo bird finally gives up the unequal struggle to survive, in the face of man and the animals imported to its native islands, and becomes extinct.

1700 Joseph Sauveur explains and measures the vibrations of musical tones.

Musical Scales

properly known. A number of sub-genres soon evolved. Of these, the *tragédie lyrique*, or *tragédie en musique*, was the most important. Lully's most famous operas are *Alceste* (1674), *Atys* (1676), *Thésée* (1675), and *Armide* (1686). Although his *tragédies lyriques* were given a run for their money by the lighter, more populist *opéra-ballet*, they were performed in France long after his death.

IN THE SHADE

While Lully was alive, one immensely talented composer, *Marc-Antoine*
CHARPENTIER (1643–1704), suffered from the favors his rival enjoyed. Charpentier's patrons boasted some pretty important people, including the Dauphin, but he consistently had to take second prize. It wasn't until 1693, well after Lully's death, that Charpentier's masterpiece, *Médée* – a work of Wagnerian scope whose depth makes it far richer than anything Lully ever wrote – was performed by the Académie Royale. Other important dramatic works include *David et Jonathas* (1688), written for the Jesuits and held up by some as the world's first gay opera.

PLOT SLOT

The *tragédie lyrique* was a tad formulaic. There had to be scenes of sacrifice and combat, sleep scenes (*sommeils*), and funeral scenes. There were set-pieces for chorus, compact little airs, song-and-dance routines, and grand prologues to flatter (usually) the king The drama involved amorous intrigues among – but not between – different social ranks: gods, magicians, and us mere humans. This *menu fixe* might lead the opera *ingénue* to think they are all the same. They're not.

LEFT Crowds enthralled by Lully's *Armide* as the witch-queen makes her entrance in the Paris Opera House.

1688 Plate glass is cast for the first time in France, introducing a cheap means of allowing light to enter a room while keeping the elements out.

1711 The tuning fork, a two-pronged metal instrument for checking the pitch of an instrument, is invented by English trumpeter John Shore.

1712 The last witch is executed in England; in France witches will be persecuted until 1745 and in Germany as late as 1775. It is estimated that around one million witches are put to death in Europe during this period.

1700~1765

Encore the Gallic Muse

Rameau versus Nobody

ABOVE The orchestral horn, Rameau's favorite hardware.

Many other composers of distinction carried the torch for French opera after Lully. André CAMPRA (1660–1744), Marin MARAIS (1656–1728), and Michel de MONTÉCLAIR (1667–1737) all wrote highly individual works. But it is Charpentier who most convincingly connects Lully with the next great figure of French opera, Jean-Philippe RAMEAU (1683–1764).

Five of Rameau's *tragédies lyriques* survive. The committed opera buff will take pleasure in becoming familiar with them all. They are, in order, *Hippolyte et Aricie* (1733), *Castor et Pollux* (1737), *Dardanus* (1739), *Zoroastre* (1749), and *Les Boréades* (1764). Other more or less well-known pieces in different, lighter genres are *La princesse de Navarre* (1745), *Platée* (1765), *Les fêtes de Polymnie* (1745), *Zaïs* (1748), and the one-act *Anacréon* (1754). Rameau's vibrant and fluid language was directed toward achieving a greater sense of continuity in opera, and he discarded that irrelevant appendage, the prologue, from *Zoroastre* onward.

NAMES TO NOTE

Rameau's major librettists were **Louis de Cahusac, Voltaire** *(1694–1778) and* **Jean François Marmontel** *(1723–99), though he worked with others including that immortal spinner of texts, Anon. But his first and possibly most famous opera,* Hippolyte, *was penned by the Abbé* **Simon-Joseph Pellegrin** *(1663–1745).*

LEFT *Platée,* staged by London's Royal Opera at the Edinburgh Festival in 1997, with costumes by Isaac Mizrahi.

1726 The French ballerina La Camargo makes her debut at the Paris Opéra, introducing a new, vigorous style with higher jumps.

1732 Ninepins, a game in which players bowl a ball at nine bottle-shaped pins, is played for the first time in New York.

1756 The first chocolate factory in Germany is established, but Switzerland and Belgium will go on to outshine their neighbor's product.

RIGHT Jean-Philippe Rameau in late composing mode (1760), a drawing by Louis Carmontelle.

Avant-garde

Rameau's orchestration is hugely original and imaginative, more so (some say) than his writing for voices. He imported to France instruments that that country had never known – clarinets, for instance, introduced special effects like *pizzicato* (the plucking of the strings of an otherwise bowed string instrument) in 1744 and *glissando* (sliding from note to note) in 1745. He liked contrasts, combining wind and strings more boldly than any other composer before him. If you can't handle a whole opera, sample some *divertissements* and see what I mean.

THE THREAT TO TRADITION

After its premiere in 1733, *Hippolyte* split the nation's opera-lovers into two opposing camps, the Lullistes and the Ramistes. The Lullistes (the pro-text alliance, you might call them) feared that Rameau would sweep away the traditional repertoire – i.e., operas by Lully – and worried that the musical side of opera would overwhelm the poetic side. Unfortunately for Rameau, who had a tendency to antagonize others, performers at the Opéra came down on Lully's side. The dispute lasted for several years, right through the premiere of *Dardanus* (1739). Eventually the power of Rameau's art won the day. But the episode just goes to show that the new and radical – the displacing of tradition – has always roused intense suspicion.

Today, when the operas of Monteverdi and Handel are, if not common currency, then at least acceptable tender in many opera houses, Rameau's music is not given the attention it merits. He is one of the great composers and surely deserves better.

1683 In Vienna the first coffee houses open, soon establishing a vogue that is followed in London and Paris.

1702 Royal approval from Queen Anne gives the go-ahead for horse-racing for cash reward – it will remain a royal sport for centuries.

1705 English physiologist Stephen Hales proves that plants need air, as well as water, to thrive.

1670~1750

Hamburgers with Relish
The Beginnings of German Opera

ABOVE Georg Philip "Prolific" Telemann, not an *echt* Hamburger but still a big player on the German opera scene.

With composers of Italian opera such as Johann Hasse, Niccolò Jommelli, and Antonio Caldara working in Dresden, Stuttgart, and Vienna, and the great Italian librettist Pietro METASTASIO (1698–1782) installed as Viennese court poet, imported art long held sway in Austro-Germany. Nevertheless, there were early attempts at establishing a vernacular art. Heinrich SCHÜTZ (1585–1672) tried in 1627, with his Dafne *(now lost). So did many others of lesser stature. So proud were the German-speaking people of their language that in Vienna German was used in the context of otherwise Italian works for comic effect.*

But far in the north, in Hamburg, a more permanent vernacular operatic genre was quietly being born, specifically in the Theater am Gänsemarkt, where from the late 1670s until almost the middle of the 1700s performances were mainly of works written in, or adapted for, the German language. Only one important Hamburg-born composer, *Johann MATTHESON* (1681–1764), was involved. He wrote an opera called *Boris Goudenov*, not to be confused with Mussorgsky's opera of the same name.

Among the non-Hamburgers there were Handel, who composed *Almira, Nero, Florindo,* and *Daphne* (all in German) in 1704–5; the notoriously prolific, but really rather good *Georg Philip TELEMANN* (1681–1767); and the most important of this group – qualitatively and quantitively – *Reinhard KEISER* (1674–1739).

LEFT Dashing costume design from Handel's *Agrippina* (1709), written in Venice during one of his Italian intervals.

1706 Dick Turpin, famed English highwayman and scourge of the rich, is born.

1724 Gin (from the Dutch word for juniper), first distilled in The Netherlands, becomes popular in England – it will have to wait another 134 years for its essential counterpart, tonic, to be patented in London.

1738 Joseph Guillotin, a French physician who will lend his name to the beheading device that will terrorize the aristocracy during the French Revolution, is born.

SINGING ACTORS

What came next was the evolution of *Singspiel* – a peculiarly Germanic, populist form, partly influenced by English ballad opera, of which more later. First established in Vienna, *Singspiel* mixed spoken text with sung text and included a strong comic element. Most of the singers were actors who could sing a bit, so early *Singspiel* is really a precursor of the musical. The best early composer was *Johann Adolph Hiller* (1728–1804), but you would have to go a long way to see anything by him on the stage these days. But *Singspiel* was to have a telling influence.

Oper and Opera

What was different about German opera, apart from the language? Well, the arias were shorter, less fancy than the Italian kind, though oddly they were sometimes sung in Italian anyway. The drama – based on the same kind of subjects as later seventeenth-century Italian operas – was considered pre-eminent. There were no fancy singers, and certainly no imported castrati, to distract the audience from the real matter in hand.

RIGHT Johann Mattheson, singer, composer and Handel's temperamental duelling buddy.

NAMES TO NOTE

Reinhard Keiser *wrote scores of opera scores: Handel thought enough of* Claudius *(1703),* Octavia *(1705), and other works to borrow from them. But the real masterworks are* Masagniello *(1706, revised in 1727 by Telemann),* Ulysses *(1722), and* Croesus *(1710). And we never see, or hear, any of them. Better news with* **Telemann's** *best operas.* Orpheus *(1726) has French influence;* Socrates *(1721) brilliantly shows off the wind section of the Hamburg orchestra; and* Pimpinone *(1728) anticipates later developments in the field of opera buffa (see p.30).* **Mattheson's** *music was largely destroyed, but* Cleopatra *(1704) suggests that he was a composer of individuality, influenced by folk music.*

❝ ⭐ ❞

Artistic Differences

An argument between Handel, directing from the harpsichord, and Mattheson, singing the part of Antony at one performance of *Cleopatra*, led to a duel between the two young men. The story goes that Handel's life was saved by a strategically positioned button, and thereafter M. and H. resumed a close friendship.

1702 Pantomime (from the Greek word meaning "all imitating") is given in its earliest form at Drury Lane, London. Over the years it will change radically, from mimed episode in a larger work to farcical stage show traditionally shown at Christmas time.

1714 The fine-pointed syringe is invented by French surgeon Dominique Anel. Three years later Lady Mary Wortley Montagu introduces smallpox inoculation.

1716 Lancelot "Capability" Brown, the English landscape gardener with eternal enthusiasm for the "capabilities" of natural landscapes, is born.

1710~1726

The German, the Italian, and the Brit
Mr. Handel Comes to Town

ABOVE George Frideric Handel, the German who found lasting fame in England.

London town, that is. As we saw, the young HANDEL (1685–1759) first made his mark in Hamburg. Then he went south, to Rome. His language evolved into something more cosmopolitan, his brilliance began to dazzle, and he honed his technique to perfection, writing a couple of operas on the way. In September 1710 he paid his first visit to London, where he composed his debut Italian opera for England. The work was Rinaldo, *given its premiere on 24 February 1711. It stayed in rep until June and indelibly stamped Handel's mark on English musical life.*

After a brief sojourn in Germany, Handel was back in London by the autumn of 1712, on the condition of his patron, the Elector of Hanover, that he didn't stay too long. He ended up working there for the rest of his life. Four operas – *Il pastor fido* (1712), *Teseo* (1713), *Silla* (1713), and *Amadigi di Gaula* (1715) – were written soon after his return. Then Handel was appointed Master, "with a Sallary [*sic*]," of the Orchestra of the newly formed Royal Academy of Music, a movement begun by the king and supported by the nobility to establish Italian opera in London on a permanent basis. For its opening 1720 season Handel wrote *Radamisto.* This work opened the floodgates.

RIGHT Handel's organ was installed in the New Covent Garden Theatre in 1734, where many of his works were staged. The theater burned down in 1808.

1717 Handel's "Water Music," allegedly written for a royal water party to restore the composer to favor with King George I, is performed on the River Thames.

1720 Wallpaper becomes a fashionable decorating accessory in England.

1726 Charles Burney, English organist, music historian, and father of the diarist Fanny Burney, is born.

The Defenestration Episode

Perhaps the story that says most about Handel's temperament (not to mention that of opera singers) concerns his star singer Francesca Cuzzoni (c.1700–70). According to Handel's biographer, Cuzzoni refused to sing the aria "Falsa imagine" in Handel's *Ottone*, in which she was making her London stage debut. Handel's response: *"Oh! Madame, je sais bien que vous êtes une véritable Diablesse: mais je vous ferais savoir, moi, que je suis Beelzebub, le Chef des Diables"* ("Madam, I know very well that you are a veritable She-devil; but I would have you know that I am Beelzebub, Chief of Devils"). With this he lifted the singer up by the waist and swore that, if she said anything else, he would fling her bodily right out of the window. The thought of a difficult and arrogant prima donna being dangled from a first-story window is almost too delicious to be disbelieved, so let's take it on board.

NAMES TO NOTE

The obstreperous Cuzzoni had to contend with a better-natured rival, **Faustina Bordoni** *(1700–81), and the two of them formed a powerful chemistry onstage with the castrato* **"Senesino"** *(c.1680–1759, aka Francesco Bernardi). Other singers whom Handel invited to England included the contralto* **Margherita Durastanti** *(c.1685–1734); the bass* **Antonio Montagnana** *(fl.1730–50); the sopranos* **Anna Maria Strada** *(?– before 1773) and* **Celeste Gismondi** *(d.1735); and the castrati* **Carlo Scalzi** *(fl.1719–38) and* **Giovanni Carestini** *(c.1705– c.1760).*

The following season, with fellow-Academy composers Giovanni Bononcini and Filippo Amadei, Handel took part in composing *Muzio Scevola* – they wrote one act each – and the season after that penned *Floridante*. There followed *Ottone* and *Flavio* (1723), then a stream of masterpieces: *Giulio Cesare in Egitto* and *Tamerlano* (both 1724), *Rodelinda* (1725), then *Scipione* and *Alessandro* (both 1726). These works took Handel's version of the Italian art to new heights. Though based on the conventions of *opera seria*, their boundaries were blurred, their forms distorted to suit the ebb and flow of the music. Dramatic pacing and depth of characterization were paramount and complex psyches were laid bare. No composer of the time could see into his characters' souls as deeply as Handel.

1736 The first successful operation for appendicitis is performed.

1740 "Rule, Britannia!," beloved theme tune of British patriots, appears in the masque *Alfred* by Thomas Arne. It is later taken up by Handel, Beethoven, and Wagner.

1745 Bonnie Prince Charlie, the Young Pretender, invades England to claim the throne but is routed and forced to flee. He wanders the Highlands with the price of £30,000 on his head, before escaping back to France.

1727~1740

Enter Mack the Knife
Handel Goes Down Fighting

ABOVE Exciting, sexy, violent, and sung in English – John Gay's *Beggar's Opera* swaggered into town and wiped the floor with the operatic opposition.

The Academy's pre-eminence did not last long. Despite three fine new Handel operas, Riccardo Primo *(1727),* Siroe *(1728, his first setting of Metastasio), and* Tolomeo *(1728), subscriptions dwindled in the 1727–8 season, and on 1 June 1728 the company closed down with a performance of* Admeto. *Meanwhile, down the road at Lincoln's Inn Fields, a work was filling the theater night after night. It was a ballad opera by John GAY (1685–1732) called* The Beggar's Opera, *first given on 29 January 1728. Ballad opera – a populist mix of well-known songs – was to be fashionable for the next 10 years or so. Those English composers who attempted to emulate Handel (men like John Frederick Lampe and Thomas Arne) had very limited success. Opera in English was now all the rage.*

But Handel was not a man to go down without a fight. Together with the assistant manager at the Haymarket, Johann Jakob Heidegger, he created the Second Academy (1729). Two new operas, *Lotario* (1729) and *Partenope* (1730), failed to bring the crowds back, however, despite a radical change in the latter from lofty, heroic drama to pointed comedy. *Poro* (1731) seemed to change the tide in his favor, but *Ezio*, the following year, was a disaster, and for his next opera, *Sosarme* (1732), Handel was obliged to cut out the recitatives.

Oratorio

Many people get confused about what is opera and what is oratorio. Handel wrote both, and was always quite clear about

ABOVE An oratorio; the sacred theme is a giveaway.

which was which. Oratorio is best defined as a form usually based on a sacred text involving singers (solo and/or chorus) and orchestra that tells a story but does not enact it (unlike opera). The real fathers of the oratorio form are Giacomo Carissimi (1605–74) and Luigi Rossi (c.1597–1653). Handel re-invented and anglicized oratorio, *Messiah* (1742) being his most famous (Hallelujah!). Some of his oratorios – *Susannah* (1749) and *Theodora* (1750) among them – are more operatic in nature, though not intent. Go hear.

1749 Handel's Music for the Royal Fireworks comes in with a bang in London's Green Park, to mark the Peace of Aix-la-Chapelle.

1750 The population of Europe is now estimated to be approximately 140 million.

1758 The manufacture of hose (garment, not water pipe) is transformed by the invention of a ribbing machine.

THE TIDE TURNS

Audiences at Italian operas wanted arias, even if that meant the storyline becoming well nigh incomprehensible. Something had to give. Handel was still to write many great Italian operas – *Orlando* (1733), *Arianna in Creta* (1734), *Ariodante* (1735), *Alcina* (1735), *Serse* (1738), and *Imeneo* (1740) – but the machinations of a rival company, the Opera of the Nobility, backed by the Prince of Wales, were a constant threat, and in any case public taste had changed. Italian opera in London was dying on its feet. Handel had to adapt…

And he did, brilliantly, by inventing the new genre of English oratorio.

Pop Music?

With *The Beggar's Opera*, arranged by the composer Johann Christoph Pepusch (1667–1752), John Gay changed London's operatic scene forever. Here was an art form that was understandable and had a moral message, and whose music was simplistic and familiar. Despite its enormous popularity, Gay was never able to repeat his success. The satire of *Polly*, its sequel (which was directed against Robert Walpole, the English Prime Minister), was felt to be too close to reality.

RIGHT Handel's secret weapon, the oratorio, soon caught on. *The Messiah* is here shown in performance at Drury Lane Theatre in a cartoon by John Nixon (1814).

NAMES TO NOTE · NAMES TO NOTE

After Gay's effort, ballad operas, which were likely to contain as "arias" songs from diverse sources, became almost two-a-penny in London for about seven years. They might be on historical themes (Walter Aston's The Restauration of King Charles II*) or classical spoofs (such as John Motley and Thomas Cooke's* Penelope*). But such pieces were really only supporting acts in theaters. After Gay, the most successful author of ballad opera texts was* **Henry Fielding** *(1707–54, he of* Tom Jones *fame), whose works – many written explicitly for Kitty Clive at Drury Lane – became staples of the repertoire until the end of the eighteenth century. Otherwise the fad was short-lived, although its effect upon British music drama was long-term.*

NAMES TO NOTE · NAMES TO NOTE

1705 Carlo Broschi Farinelli, the great Italian castrato singer, is born. He will become such a favorite that women faint from excitement at his performances and the melancholy Philip V offers him 50,000 francs a year to remain in Madrid and cheer him up. Farinelli agrees and for the next 25 years sings the same four songs every night.

1709 The modern piano is invented, when the great Italian harpsichord maker Bartolomeo de Francesco Cristofori constructs a *gravicembali col piano e forte.*

1728 Danish navigator Vitus Bering proves that there is sea between Siberia and Alaska by sailing straight through it – it will become known as the Bering Strait.

1700~1750
Opera in Arcadia
Metastasio and the Serious Side

Despite Handel et al., Italian opera was still being composed and performed in Italy itself. Alessandro SCARLATTI (1660–1725), doyen of Italian opera composers at the end of the seventeenth century, had brought to its fullest flowering the da capo *form of aria. Strings, rather than just a simple continuo group, now accompanied arias. And Scarlatti's overtures settled into the fast-slow-fast, three-movement shape that was to metamorphose within half a century or so into the classical symphony.*

ABOVE Metastasio, prodigious poet and librettist extraordinaire; some of his texts were used more than 60 times.

Since Monteverdi, Italian opera had become increasingly colorful. Some began to think it had gone too far and that some purifying had now become necessary. So evolved the notion of *opera seria*. No funny bits. No extremes. No surfeit of dazzling machinery. No digressions. And a regular structure. It was a literary-dominated current. The most famous *opera seria* librettist was *Pietro METASTASIO* (1698–1782), who was born Antonio Trapassi and adopted by a wealthy Roman scholar, who educated him, gave him his new name, and left him sufficient funds to pursue a literary career.

1740 The 8-year-old Franz Joseph Haydn becomes a choirboy at St. Stephen's in Vienna; when his voice breaks at 17, he is plunged into poverty.

1746 The wearing of tartans is forbidden in Great Britain. The clan cloth will not come into its checkered own again until another 35 years have elapsed.

1749 Sign language for deaf mutes, using hand and finger movements, is invented by the Portuguese Giacobbo Rodriguez Pereire.

Arcadia

Metastasian operas are often set in Arcadia, a kind of virtual countryside that symbolized Innocence and Nature (as opposed to the wicked worldliness of Town). It's all the fault of the poet Sir Philip Sidney, who used it as the title of a romance written for the Countess of Pembroke in 1590. Actually, Arcadia really exists. It's a place in Greece named after Arcas, son of Jupiter. The Arcadian Academy was founded in Rome in 1689 to oppose the artificiality of seventeenth-century Italian art, and spread naturally enough to music – Il pastor fido (see p.24) was supposedly the pastoral libretto par excellence.

INTRIGUE AND INNER STRUGGLE

Metastasio's approach, shown in his libretto for *Didone abbandonata* (1724) for instance, is rational, dignified, conservative. Is he boring? Well, no. His characters become involved in intrigues and moral dilemmas and usually emerge happier and better people for the experience. Their inner wrestlings are excuses for composers and singers to indulge in virtuosic excess. The format might be standardized – six or seven characters, divided into two groups of primary and secondary importance, fair allocation and distribution of arias, an exit aria at the end of each scene – but in Metastasio's hands, each plot had its own individuality. And dozens of composers responded to his unarguably sweet poetry.

LEFT Shepherds puzzle over the ominous inscription in Poussin's *Et in Arcadia Ego*; the Ego who is also in Arcadia is, of course, Death, who attends every feast.

Metastasian Composers

Three generations treated Metastasio's texts. From 1720 to 1740 the dominant composers were Leonardo Vinci (1690–1730), Leonardo Leo (1694–1744), Nicola Porpora (1686–1768), Johann Adolph Hasse (1699–1783), and Giovanni Battista Pergolesi (1710–36), whose *L'Olimpiade* has been cited as a fine Arcadian opera. From 1740 until about 1770 Hasse was joined by Niccolò Jommelli (1714–44), Baldassare Galuppi (1706–85), and Johann Christian Bach (1735–82), who wrote two Metastasian operas for Naples and one for Turin – thus qualifying as a temporarily adoptive Italian. Jommelli was chastized by Metastasio for introducing indulgent elements. From 1770 until 1800 the major Metastasian opera composers were Niccolò Piccinni (1728–1800), Antonio Salieri (1750–1825, Mozart's colleague), Giovanni Paisiello (1740–1816), and Domenico Cimarosa (1749–1801).

1756 Italian adventurist, spy, librarian, violinist, and (incidentally) great lover, Casanova de Seingalt escapes from the "Piombi" in Venice.

1766 The Tsarina Catherine the Great grants freedom of worship in Russia – it will wax and wane like the moon over the next two centuries.

1770 William Wordsworth, who will immortalize a host of golden daffodils, is born at Cockermouth in England.

1700~1800
Opera Buffa
The Funny Men

ABOVE Domenico Cimarosa (1749–1801), Neopolitan *opera buffa* king.

Parallel to Metastasian opera seria *ran its opposite,* opera buffa, *or comic opera. Unlike any other European comic opera, it was entirely set to music. It too had its conventions – the cast numbered between six and about nine, for instance. It was intended to instruct through caricature. The first* opera buffa *proper was Michelangelo FAGGIOLI's* La Cilla, *written in Naples in 1706. The Teatro dei Fiorentini became the first theater in Naples to offer* opera buffa *regularly, starting in 1709 with Antonio OREFICE's Patrò Calienno della Costa. (Yes, he really was called Orefice.)*

Opera buffa spread rapidly throughout Europe, and even intellectuals began to take it seriously. Whereas in *opera seria* the singers were chiefly concerned with their own singing, in *opera buffa* (as in German *Singspiel*), they were actors first, singers second. It showed in their impeccable comic timing and in the irrepressible flow of the drama. And the potential market was wider than that for *opera seria*. *Opera buffa* could caricature trends in literature or drama; it could respond to the political intrigues and scandals of the day. It was irreverent, not straitjacketed or formal, though this did not mean that it was also unsophisticated. Most of the finest composers of *opera buffa* were the same musicians as those who composed fine *opera seria* – variety being the spice of any working life.

PLOT SLOT

Like *opera seria*, *opera buffa* developed a two-tier cast. One set of singers took the *parti buffe*, the roles of the funny people; the other set was responsible for the *parti serie*, the serious people. Their presence lent a subtlety to the equation of humor and seriousness. In Mozart's mature operas, such as *Don Giovanni*, many characters show aspects of both *buffa* and *seria* roles.

ABOVE Character from Goldoni's *Battista*.

1782 Niccolò Paganini, Italian violinist and composer, is born a porter's son in Genoa. His Mephistophelean appearance arouses rumors that his virtuoso performances stem from diabolical powers.

1793 French physician Philippe Pinel, put in charge of an asylum, strikes the chains off its inmates and declares that those sick in mind deserve to be treated as well as those sick in body. Such a humane outlook will take half a century to be adopted elsewhere in Europe.

1799 A perfectly preserved mammoth is discovered in Siberia.

SERIOUSLY WIDESPREAD

In 1724, Naples' Nuovo and Pace theaters opened their portals to *buffo* works, from which time some "serious" composers tried their hand at it. Rome became a center from the 1730s: *Gaetano* LATILLA's *La finta cameriera* (originally *Il Gismondo*, 1737) came there in 1738, then went on a triumphant procession all round the country and even to northern Europe during the next ten years. Later in the century Venice took over the mantle. *Baldassare* GALUPPI's *La forza d'amore* (1745) was the first *opera buffa* by a Venetian composer to make its mark. Mozart's *Le nozze di Figaro*, *Don Giovanni* and *Così fan tutte* (see pp.38–41) represent the very summit of eighteenth-century *opera buffa*.

TO NOTE — NAMES

Baldassare Galuppi, Leonardo Vinci, *and* **Leonardo Leo** *should all feature in the erudite opera-lover's name-dropping list. So should Neapolitans* **Domenico Cimarosa** *(whose best-known work is* Il matrimonio segreto *of 1792) and* **Giovanni Paisiello.**

BELOW Salzburg's delicious 1982 staging of Mozart's *Così fan tutte*, the *crema di opera buffa*.

Carlo Goldoni, the Comedy King

Although he did not entirely dominate the market, the most celebrated *opera buffa* librettist was the Venetian Carlo Goldoni (1707–93), who was even more famous as a prolific and popular comic dramatist (250 greatest hits). He was enlisted as librettist by Galuppi. *L'Arcadia in Brenta* (1749), *Il mondo della luna* (1750), *La calamità de" cuori* (1752), *Il filosofo di campagna* (1754), and *La diavolessa* (1755) were among the collaborations that were immense successes far beyond Venice.

1749 Italian composer Domenico Cimarosa is born. His *Il matrimonia segreto* will be so successful that at the first performance Leopold II will have supper served to the cast before the performance is repeated.

1751 The first volume of Denis Diderot's massive undertaking, the *Encyclopédie*, is published. Despite the threat of imprisonment or exile, due to its enlightened social and political views, Diderot sticks by his task to see all 35 volumes published.

1752 In adopting the Gregorian calendar, Britain loses the days 3–13 September 1752; landlords, however, still charge rent for the missing 11 days.

1750~1755

Opera Politica
The Querelle des Bouffons

ABOVE Jean-Jacques Rousseau in his prime, surrounded by his philosophical *œuvres*.

The quarrel of the hairstyles? Not exactly. The Querelle (or Guerre) des Bouffons was a dispute that simmered, bubbled, and boiled in Paris between 1752 and 1754. It was ostensibly about the relative merits of French and Italian opera. And it took the form of an exchange of pamphlets, the first of them between the philosopher-writers Friedrich von Grimm and Jean-Jacques Rousseau in January 1753. All the leading French philosophers, including Denis Diderot and Jean le Rond D'Alembert, became involved in the dispute.

Why "Bouffons?" That was the name given to an Italian troupe who had come to Paris to perform Pergolesi's *La serva padrona* in the summer of 1752. They were, of course, innocent bystanders.

In reality, the *Querelle* was not just about opera, but was part of a wholesale political crisis. In May 1753 members of the Paris *parlement* had been exiled by Louis XV for ignoring his edict forbidding them to sue the Archbishop of Paris over his actions in a dispute between two factions in the Church. (Still with us?) The parliamentarians were challenging the monarchy's absolutism, of which opera was one manifestation, so an attack on the opera establishment was part of that challenge.

Liberté, Egalité, Fraternité!

Jean-Jacques Rousseau (1712–78), radical philosopher *extraordinaire*, inspirer of the Romantic movement, boldly argued in a 1749 essay that arts and sciences merely corrupted

ABOVE Rousseau *enchaîné*.

people's natural goodness. Thenceforward in his writings he developed the theme of the "noble savage," plus associated political ideas: it is (human-made) institutions that have corrupted people's freedom, equality and goodness, he says. And the famous opening words of his *Contrat social* (1762) – "Man is born free; and everywhere he is in chains" – have become emblematic of the essential dichotomies between the human condition and government. Chew on that one, if you will.

1752 After flying a kite with a metal point in a thunderstorm (and living to tell the tale), Benjamin Franklin invents the lightning conductor. First America and then Europe adopts his lightning rods, which rely for the first time on natural laws, rather than prayer or magic.

1753 The Marriage Act forbids weddings by unauthorized persons in Britain.

1755 Marie Antoinette, whose taunt, "Let them eat cake," will help precipitate the French Revolution, is born. She will, however, get her come-uppance in due course.

THE KING'S CORNER
V. THE QUEEN'S CORNER

The supporters of French opera (who included Madame de Pompadour, the court and the aristocracy) were called the *coin du roi*, from their habit of gathering by the King's box; they admired the close link between words and music in French opera and decried the fancy arias in Italian opera. The pro-Italians (including the Queen and numerous intellectuals) were dubbed the *coin de la reine* and ridiculed the artifice, complexity, and lack of melody in French opera, pointing to Italian opera's graceful melodic charms. The argument basically centered on which – music or text – was more important.

And the result? The Bouffons went on their way. The Opéra produced *tragédies lyriques* for another two decades. But by the late 1750s a new generation of composers began writing *opéra comique*, which soon became at least as popular as its loftier rival form.

BELOW Sumptuous command performance in the Argentine Theater, Rome, ordered by Louis XV to celebrate the wedding of his only son, Louis the Dauphin.

1722 On Easter Sunday a Dutch navigator comes across one of the most isolated bits of land in the world. Easter Island mystifies visitors with its 600 enigmatic stone statues of a type found nowhere else on Earth.

1731 Johann Hasse becomes Kapellmeister at the Dresden Opera, although he is plagued by rivalries and jealousies; his wife, Faustina Bordoni, conveniently becomes its prima donna.

1732 Covent Garden Opera House in London, formerly a convent garden, opens to a rather more vociferous audience with Congreve's play *The Way of the World*.

1740~1790
Vienna to Paris and Back Again
Gluck the Reformer

ABOVE Christoph Gluck pictured at his spinet in 1775, soon after his move to Vienna.

After writing eight successful operas in Italy (1741–5), two unsuccessful operas for London (1745–6), and going through an itinerant phase, Christoph Willibald GLUCK (1714–87) settled in Vienna in 1752.

It was a good place to be. The imperial poet was the opera seria librettist Metastasio. And the broad-minded Intendant of the Viennese theaters, Count Durazzo, imported the new-fangled opéras comiques from Paris, to which Gluck often added his own arias and overtures. He even composed eight opéras comiques by himself and wrote the revolutionary ballet score Don Juan (1761), which comprised a dramatic ballet d'action, rather than the conventional divertissement en dance. Its premiere caused shockwaves, but it soon won over Vienna's naturally progressive audiences.

Durazzo was keen to combine French and Italian elements in opera, so when the poet *Raniero de CALZABIGI* (1714–95) arrived in the city, the Intendant sensed the perfect partnership. Calzabigi went on to write the librettos for Gluck's *opera serie Orfeo ed Euridice* (1762), *Alceste* (1767), and *Paride ed Elena* (1770).

1744 "God Save the Queen" (or "King"!) is published in *Thesaurus Musicus*. The tune is borrowed by about 20 other countries as their national song – in the American colonies it becomes "God Save America," "God Save George Washington" and even, catchily, "God Save the Thirteen States."

1760 Portsmouth dockyard in England is destroyed by fire.

1762 Mozart, already a musical prodigy, having played the klavier at the age of three and started composing at five, tours Europe at the age of six, now playing the violin without having had any formal teaching.

BELOW An inattentive audience pose before a performance of Gluck's *Il Parnaso confuso* (1765, book by P. Metastasio).

FUEL FOR THE FIRE

Gluck took his ideas to the Paris Opéra, offering a new work, *Iphigénie en Aulide*, to show just what he could do. After much hassle, entailing re-training of singers and endless rehearsals, *Iphigénie*'s first performance in April 1774 was a triumph. Thereafter, Gluck made French versions of *Orfeo* (1774) and *Alceste* (1776) and wrote more new works for Paris. He was still in demand in Vienna, so he traveled to and fro. But there was something of a hiccup in 1776 when a rival composer, Niccolò Piccinni, arrived in Paris. Piccinni was working on a libretto by Philippe Quinault – *Roland* – that Gluck was also tackling. Incensed, Gluck burned his own version.

He sounds like a truly serious composer. Well, he was. For Gluck, the total experience was the only possible experience, though for all that the beauties of a favorite aria, like "Que faro senz' Euridice" from *Orfeo*, stand well in isolation.

That Famous Aria

Quite justly, "Que faro senz' Euridice" (usually translated as "What is life to me without you?") is by far the most famous aria from any of Gluck's operas and, thanks to immortal performances by Kathleen Ferrier, one of the most famous opera arias of all. What's so special about it? Its melody has grace in abundance, though it is also simple. It doesn't go too far in breast-beating and self-indulgence. And there is enough light left in the music to provide a happy ending.

RIGHT Kathleen Ferrier as Orpheus singing That Famous Aria.

Reform Opera

In *Alceste*'s preface, Gluck set out his promise to divest *opera seria* of its indulgences. Instead there would be uninterrupted sung dialogue, an overture relevant in content and proportion, less marked contrast between recitative and aria, and clarity of expression. This formula became known as reform opera, and had resonances in Mozart and even in Wagner.

1706 English inventor Henry Mill constructs carriage springs for the first time – the swaying they cause is preferable to the wild lurching and jolting of unsprung carriages.

1711 The clarinet features in J.A. Hasse's opera *Croesus*. Much later Mozart becomes the first great composer to use the single-reed instrument in a classical symphony.

1727 The first marriage advertisement in an English newspaper appears in Manchester.

1700~1790

Opéra Comique
Ha! Ha! Ha!

Evolutionary lines take weird detours. In France, as elsewhere, light-hearted, populist dramatic and musical street entertainment was a tradition stretching back probably to prehistory. The thirteenth-century composer Adam de la Halle wrote a piece called Le jeu de Robin et Marion *that interspersed music and spoken texts; and stock characters, roughly parallel to those of the Italian* commedia dell'arte, *developed.*

In the era of opera, Lully and Molière (1622–73) showed they had a sense of humor by writing *comédies-ballets* for court performance. But Lully's loftily serious *tragédies lyriques* were also ripe for parody, and comedy troupes – French and Italian – seized the opportunity with relish. When the law forbade such parodies, the troupes circumnavigated that minor difficulty by miming, displaying the text on written cards suspended from the ceiling, and installing in the audience a group – or claque – to lead the singing of the popular songs, or *vaudevilles*. In 1715 the term *opéra comique* was coined: music was still very much a secondary element, but there was one important musical innovation, the introduction of the *ariette*, a halfway house between *vaudeville* and aria.

OPÉRA COMIQUE COMES OF AGE

In 1726 two new characters were added to the stock cast – the *ingénus* country lovers. These rustic innocents elevated the *double entendre* to new heights: more refined in manner, if not in substance. Such socially acceptable veneer was important. Voltaire, no less, held that the most celebrated *opéra comique* librettist, Charles Simon Favart, was responsible for turning the form into something fit for decent people. Now it had come of age and was ready to rival the pre-eminence of the old-fashioned

LEFT All the fun of the *foire*: alfresco theaters were a feature of 18th-century street fairs.

1736 "India rubber," or hard rubber caoutchouc, is brought to England.

1760 English physicist John Michell establishes that earthquakes occur in volcanic areas, traveling through the rocks beneath the sea, and are not in fact caused by gods or demons imprisoned underground.

1783 The paper-making Montgolfier brothers make the first successful flight in a hot-air balloon for 20 minutes above Paris.

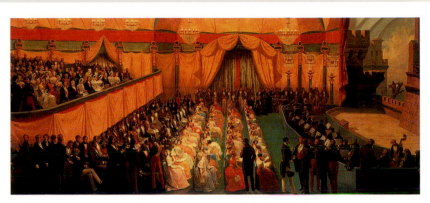

ABOVE *Richard the Lionheart,* composed by the Belgian André Grétry and performed in a marquee in an attempt to amuse a young Queen Victoria.

tragédie lyrique. Rousseau's words and music for *Le devin du village*, composed in the wake of the eruption of the *Querelle des Bouffons*, clinched it. Now opera could be about normal, humble beings, rather than gods and kings. For the next 50 years, *opéra comique* ruled the roost, and became less and less funny. Then along came a famous Belgian, *André GRÉTRY* (1741–1813), who arrived in Paris in 1767.

Grétry was no Mozart. Even he admitted he wasn't the world's greatest composer. But he did have a gift for writing straightforward, characterful melodies, and for creating some neat orchestral effects. Over a period of three decades he wrote more than 40 *opéras comiques* of various hues. They even included an unlikely celebration of royalty, *Richard Coeur de Lion* (written in 1784, only five years before the French Revolution), an

TO NOTE — NAMES — NAMES — TO NOTE — TO NOTE — NAMES — NAMES — TO NOTE

There were even important composers of opéra comique. **François–André Danican Philidor** *(1726–95), also a renowned chess player, wrote fine works based on stories by La Fontaine, Cervantes, Perrault, and Henry Fielding (the author of* Tom Jones *of 1765). The librettist Michel-Jean Sedaine cemented an alliance with the composer* **Pierre Alexandre Monsigny** *(1729–1817) in the creation of an* opéra comique *that dealt with serious issues of social injustice. In Monsigny's and Sedaine's* Le déserteur *(1769), comic elements are mere sideshows,*

early rescue opera whose hero, Blondel, has his own theme, anticipating Wagner's leitmotiv technique by some 50 years. Grétry also composed a *Guillaume Tell* (1792) well before Rossini, throwing into it some extravagantly vivid battle music. No Mozart, maybe; but no fool, either.

1756 Wolfgang Amadeus Mozart is born in Salzburg and christened with the memorable name Johannes Chrysostomus Wolfgangus Theophilus – no wonder he wants a shorter version.

1760 French wax-modeller Marie ("Madame") Tussaud is born. During the French Revolution she and her uncle will take death masks of many victims and leaders – useful in her London exhibition of celebrities and its Chamber of Horrors.

1764 The practice of numbering houses is introduced for the first time in London, while a couple of years later the first pavement is laid in Central London.

1750~1790

Mozart's Famous Operas: Part One
Figaro and *The Don*

Most people accept that Wolfgang Amadeus MOZART (1756–91) wrote four great operas. Most people are mistaken about this, because there's nothing less great about operas like Die Entführung aus dem Serail *or* Idomeneo *(turn over a couple of pages for the lowdown). But back to those four operas:* Le nozze di Figaro, Don Giovanni, Così fan tutte *(libretti by Lorenzo DA PONTE, 1749–1838) and* Die Zauberflöte *(libretto by Emanuel SCHIKANEDER, 1751–1812). In all three Da Ponte works, Mozart brilliantly, and endearingly, points out the unreliability of human beings.*

L*e nozze di Figaro*, first seen in Vienna in 1786, is a masterpiece of bristling, intricate comedy in which Count Almaviva mistreats his wife and lusts after a maid, Susanna, who is betrothed to his servant Figaro. The plot concerns Figaro's revenge and exposure of the hypocritical, but ultimately penitent, Count.

Mozart's Journeys

From boyhood, Mozart got around. He went to Mannheim four times: the reputation of the musical establishment at the Bavarian Elector's court was impressive. All Mozart's operas were given early first performances in the Elector's palace there. Paris also had a great effect on Mozart's style: boldness, breadth, and confidence, along with a particular kind of elegance, grace his 1778 Parisian pieces. Prague was a later destination in 1787. There was an outburst of Mozartmania when he arrived, and the impressario Bondini commissioned Mozart to compose *Don Giovanni; La clemenza di Tito* was another, later Prague commission.

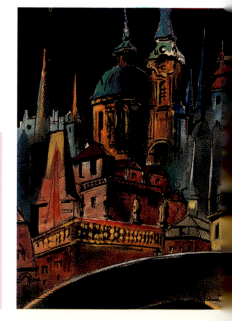

1767 Taxes are imposed on tea, glass, paper and dyestuffs in the American colonies – protest ensues at Boston, which will in due course turn into a Tea Party.

1770 In Hungary, an opal of nearly 3,000 carats is discovered.

1772 The first barrel organs, in which projections on a hand-rotated barrel bring the notes into play, is made by the London firm of Flight and Kelly.

Man and Superman

The Don Juan story has inspired many an artist, but perhaps the most original version was that made by playwright and critic George Bernard Shaw. In his *Man and Superman*, the action is boldly translated to modern times and the anti-hero dreams his Hell scene, arguing with the Devil, the statue, and his would-be lover Ann (in the guise of Donna Anna).

ABOVE George Bernard Shaw, author of *Man and Superman*.

BELOW Vaclav Pavlik's menacing set for Act IV of *Don Giovanni* in the 1929 production by the National Theater of Prague.

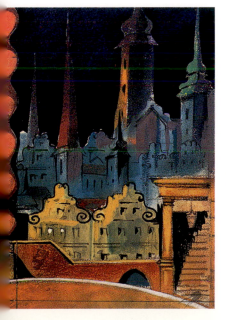

HELL AND DAMNATION

Don Giovanni, first performed in Prague in 1787, is a complex work of comedy and horror. It opens with attempted rape and a killing. But Giovanni's servant, Leporello, is a figure of fun, and there's a cute young peasant couple, with the peasant girl Zerlina pleading with her boyfriend Masetto to beat her till she's black and blue. *Chacun à son gout*, as they say in France. And finally the incredible finale: the murder victim's statue comes to dinner with Giovanni, terrifying the life out of Leporello and contributing a just dessert to the feast – Giovanni's consignment to Hell.

ABOVE Figaro, the table-turning valet to the libidinous Count Almaviva and star of Mozart's *Le nozze de Figaro*.

It is no coincidence that *Figaro*'s and *Don Giovanni*'s villains are noblemen, nor that by the end of both operas all social classes are united in a justice they have helped bring about. Mozart himself had problems with the nobility – most notoriously with the Archbishop of Salzburg – refusing to play the part of servant at a time when musicians were treated as such. And in these operas he thumbs his nose at class distinctions and points a gently accusatory finger at the foibles of human beings.

1768 English chemist Joseph Priestley, while living next door to a brewery, uses the carbon dioxide it creates to make a refreshing drink – soda water – so becoming the father of the giant soft-drinks industry.

1774 The curious rules of cricket are drawn up for the first time.

1778 La Scala opens in Milan to replace the Royal Ducal Theater, which had burned down two years before – every great Italian composer will write for it and the theater will reach its zenith under the baton of Arturo Toscanini.

1790~1791

Mozart's Famous Operas: Part Two
Così and *Flute*

ABOVE Fan, flute, genius: Mozart.

The six-strong cast of Così fan tutte *(1790) is made up of social equals, with the exception of the minx-like maid, Despina. Two male friends strike up a wager with the cynical Don Alfonso that if they were to part from their sweethearts, said sweethearts would remain faithful. Stuff and nonsense, says Alfonso. And sets about proving himself right. Besides pointing out the fickleness of women, Mozart also lays bare the boorish arrogance and pathetic rivalries of men. He holds up a mirror to his audience.*

Die Zauberflöte (1791), or *The Magic Flute*, is a *Singspiel* – an amazing piece, full of outwardly simple, charming tunes and outwardly simple, charming characters to go with them. No Prince was ever as pure, noble, upright, and courageous as Tamino, no princess as radiant, etc., etc., as Pamina. There's a scene-stealing clown figure in the bird-catcher Papageno, who finally meets his love-match, Papagena. And for compulsive hissers, there's the evil Queen of the Night, Pamina's mother. She sings the most spectacular of operatic arias, reaching high Fs in her fury.

Da Ponte and Schikaneder
It would be hard to imagine two more different librettists. Lorenzo Da Ponte wrote brilliant librettos for the composers Vincente Martín y Soler (1754–1806), Antonio Salieri and above all Mozart, but some dubious business dealings at the end of the 1700s left him bankrupt, and he fled to New York to become a grocer, teacher, and dealer in Italian books – there's nothing like versatility! Emanuel Schikaneder approached his career by treading the boards. In 1780 he became friends with Mozart, and in 1788 his acting company moved to Vienna, after which came a sequence of straight plays, opera, and *Singspiel* librettos. Alas, his life ended in madness and poverty.

RIGHT Fun in Naples; lovers Fiordiligi, Ferrando, Guglielmo, and Dorabella, Don Alfonso, and the maid Despina disentangle themselves in a 1987 English production of Così.

40

1786 French doctor Michel-Gabriel Paccard and a porter are the first people to achieve the ascent of Mont Blanc, previously seen as an act of lunacy. A frenzy of mountain-climbing ensues.

1787 The dollar is adopted as currency in the U.S.A.; it will also be adopted by Australia, Canada, and Hong Kong.

1791 The year that Mozart dies, the waltz becomes popular in England.

LEFT Karl Friedrich Schinkel's set design for the palace of the Queen of the Night, wicked star of *The Magic Flute*.

What Does Così Actually Mean?

While we happily call *Le nozze di Figaro* *The Marriage of Figaro* (actually, the now-trendy *Figaro's Wedding* is more accurate, since a marriage is supposed to be for a lifetime, whereas the wedding is the fun part) and *Don Giovanni* just plain *Don Giovanni*, with *Così fan tutte* translation is more difficult. It literally means, "Thus do all," but *tutte* is feminine. So what's the solution? "All women are like that?" – a bit sexist for our times; in any case, in this opera all men are like that, too (if "that" means a touch on the gullible side). Probably best to refer to the piece simply as *Così*. What the opera tells us about human nature is more important than what it's actually called.

MASONIC CODE

But the piece has hidden depths as well as charm. It is full of secret emblems and references to Freemasonry (Mozart himself was a member of the Order). The symbolic number three features prominently – the threefold repetition of three chords in the overture, the three Ladies and three Boys, the three trials that the lovers (only two!) undergo, even the three flats in the work's home key of E flat. It has also been rumored that there is alchemic symbolism in the music. Musicals were never as sophisticated as this.

But, like all good pantomimes, *Die Zauberflöte* is an essay in morality. It stresses the virtues of courage, trust, and love. It even strikes a bold blow for feminism when Pamina is accepted as a member of the Order after undergoing the trials hand-in-hand with her beloved Tamino. Oh, and I nearly forgot – though outwardly simple and charming, the music also happens to be ravishingly beautiful.

1747 British physician James Lind realizes that citrus fruit can combat the sailor's scourge – scurvy. It's another 50 years before the British Navy can stir itself to action.

1767 Silesian composer Johann Schobert, who influenced Mozart's early keyboard works, dies with his family after eating poisonous fungi.

1793 King Louis XVI of France goes to the guillotine in the Place de la Révolution, Paris.

1780~1800

Mozart's Less Famous Operas...
and Haydn's Even Less Famous Operas

ABOVE Franz Joseph Haydn, house composer to the Esterházys.

Not every opera Mozart wrote achieved the success of the Big Four. Most people have never even heard of Lucio Silla, Mitridate, rè di Ponto, *or* Il rè pastore, *though many of these works are more than simply "clever" or "nice." But there are also three other indisputably great operas. Two of them are opera serie:* Idomeneo *(1781) is arguably Mozart's first mature opera, the closest he came to Gluck's ideal; and* La clemenza di Tito *was Mozart's very last opera, finished in 1791.*

The Esterházy Family

Haydn was a homely sort of fellow, who liked stability above all other things. That stability was provided for most of his career by the Esterházy family, who had palaces in Esterháza and at Eisenstadt. It was Prince Paul Anton who first secured Haydn's services, in 1761, but Haydn also served contentedly for almost 30 years under his son Prince Nikolaus, an avid music lover. Nikolaus's son Anton didn't like music and disbanded the orchestra, though Haydn was retained, and only four years later Anton's own son Nikolaus (this gets very confusing) revived the family's musical entourage. It was for this second Nikolaus's wife, Maria, Princess of Lichtenstein, that Haydn wrote his magnificent cycle of six late masses.

Mozart wanted to show what he could do with the old form. And he succeeded – the work was a hit for the next 20 years or so. The third great, but neglected, opera is the *Singspiel, Die Entführung aus dem Serail* (1782). All about an escape from a harem, this work is quite different from *Die Zauberflöte*, though no less involving, touching, or beautifully crafted.

RIGHT Program for Mozart's *Entführung*, described by the undereducated as an opera, when all the time it is a *Singspiel*.

1801 The Union Flag becomes the official national flag of the United Kingdom of Great Britain and Ireland.

1807 Austrian composer Ignace Pleyel founds his piano manufacturing firm, which also develops a chromatic harp and is important in the revival of interest in the harpsichord later on.

1808 Pigtails, previously *de rigueur* in men's hair, go out of fashion.

PROLIFIC HAYDN

And what about Mozart's contemporary, *Franz Joseph* HAYDN (1732–1809)? He wrote many an opera for his employers, the Esterházy family. Few are ever staged these days, which is a pity, although they aren't quite in the mature Mozart league. In any case, Haydn wasn't an instinctive man of the theater as Mozart was. He took his librettos as they were handed to him and simply wrote inventive, moving, charming music around them.

ABOVE Haydn looks on anxiously (bottom left) as the first performance of his *L'incontro improvviso* gets under way in the intimate setting of the Esterházys' court theater.

" ☆ "

Faux pas

If someone refers to *Die Entführung* as *Il Seraglio,* look pointedly at the offender. It's a German *Singspiel,* not an Italian *opera seria.*

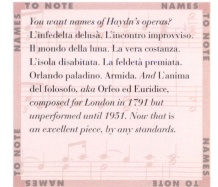

TO NOTE — NAMES

You want names of Haydn's operas? L'infedelta delusa. L'incontro improvviso. Il mondo della luna. La vera costanza. L'isola disabitata. La feldetà premiata. Orlando paladino. Armida. *And* L'anima del folosofo, *aka* Orfeo ed Euridice, *composed for London in 1791 but unperformed until 1951. Now that is an excellent piece, by any standards.*

OPERA ~ A CRASH COURSE **43**

1778 Franz Mesmer, a Viennese doctor, coins the term "animal magnetism" and causes a sensation in Paris when he practices "mesmerism."

1785 French balloonist Jean-Pierre-François Blanchard drops a dog to Earth in a basket suspended from a balloon and the parachute is born. It will be another 12 years before a human being dares attempt the same thing.

1804 Napoleon Bonaparte assumes the hereditary title of Emperor and is crowned in Paris in the presence of Pope Pius VII.

1805~1814
Beethoven's Only Opera
All Three of Them

ABOVE Ludwig van Beethoven, the musical genius who had such trouble pinning down opera.

Go on then – tell me. How many operas did Ludwig van BEETHOVEN *(1770–1827) write? You are going to say just one, aren't you?* Fidelio. *Everyone knows that. Great piece, gripping drama – a "rescue" opera about oppression, suffering, sacrifice, courage, the triumph of noble human instincts over evil, the whole works. And it's politically right-on. Beautiful girl (Leonore) has to disguise herself as a boy (Fidelio) so that she can become a prison officer and rescue her incarcerated lover (Florestan).*

You are quite right, but amazingly Beethoven found composing an opera so challenging that he had to try three times before he got it right, premiered respectively in Vienna in November 1805, May 1806, and May 1814. So why did Beethoven keep fiddling with it? And why compose it in the first place? The answer to the second question is because he was asked to, by the Theater an der Wien's director, one Emanuel Schikaneder (see p.40). Schikaneder offered a libretto of his own, which Beethoven wisely dropped in favor of J.N. Bouilly's well-known drama *Léonore*. Apparently he was preoccupied with thoughts of unjust suffering and heroism at the time. Not surprising, really – he was battling with all sorts of personal problems, not the least of which was his deafness.

RIGHT Stunning version of the Prisoners' Chorus from the *Fidelio* performed by the German State Opera in Berlin, 1996.

1810 At the Piazza in Covent Garden, London the first public billiards rooms in England are opened.

1818 Austrian schoolteacher Franz Xaver Huber writes to words of the young curate Joseph Mohr the ultimate Christmas carol, *Silent Night*.

1819 Beethoven, already afflicted by the gradual onset of incurable deafness and accompanying depression, becomes completely deaf.

THIRD TIME LUCKY

And why the revisions? The 1805 version had only three performances, partly because Vienna was occupied by the French and had been deserted by many opera-lovers. The piece was felt to be too long, so for the 1806 run Beethoven condensed it from three acts to two. Then in 1814 he was approached about a revival and took a hatchet to the opera yet again. This time scarcely a single number survived unscathed. This final, last-gasp version is now the accepted text, though its predecessors are performed from time to time. To avoid confusion with other settings of the same story, the theater insisted that the opera be called *Fidelio*.

Is it a good piece? Is the world round? There are famous great moments – the Prisoners' Chorus as they emerge into the light, the canonic Act One quartet – but the satisfaction lies in the whole. The characters aren't very deeply drawn, but neither need they be. They represent aspects of the human condition, not rounded individuals, and the work is an inner moral and psychological discourse more than a straightforward story.

Untangling the Leonora Overtures

There exist four overtures associated with Beethoven's *Fidelio*: Leonora Nos 1, 2, and 3, and the Fidelio overture itself. Leonora No. 2 came with the first (1805) version of *Leonore* (as the opera was then called). Leonora No. 3 was for version no. 2 of *Leonore* (1806). The Fidelio overture was for, well, *Fidelio* itself (1814). And Leonora No. 1 was intended for a production of the opera in Prague that never actually came about.

Other Fidelios

Beethoven's *opus magnum* didn't come entirely out of the blue. Three other notable composers of the day set the same story. There's a *Leonora* (with an "a" at the end, please note) by Ferdinando Paer (1771–1839) to an Italian libretto (hence the "a") by one Giovanni Schmidt, after Bouilly's French original, given to great acclaim in Dresden in 1804. There's a version, also in Italian, by Simone Mayr (1763–1845) called *L'amore coniugale* (1805) to a rather more liberal version of Bouilly's work by Gaetano Rossi. And there's a French *Fidelio* by Pierre Gaveaux (1760–1825), called – would you believe it? – *Léonore, ou L'amour conjugal* (also to Bouilly's original libretto), which was premiered in Paris in 1798.

1797 Merino sheep are introduced to Australia by John MacArthur.

1809 Louis Braille is born near Paris. Blind himself from the age of three, he will invent the system of raised-point writing for the blind that will take his name.

1812 Lord Byron writes *Childe Harold's Pilgrimage*. He dramatizes himself as a man of mystery, a gloomy romantic figure and gives Europe the "Byronic hero."

1810~1828

Losing the Plot
Schubert's (Mostly) Unfinished Operas

ABOVE One of Schubert's early works.

Whereas Beethoven's only opera is performed everywhere, his greatest contemporary, Franz SCHUBERT (1797–1828), is not known as a composer of opera at all. That isn't because he didn't write them. In fact, he made many attempts. The trouble was that too often Schubert seemed to get so far and no farther whenever he tackled anything longer than one act.

There are exceptions: the heroic romantic opera *Fierabras* (1823, but not performed until 1897), *Alfonso und Estrella*, written to a libretto by his friend F. von Schober (1822, but not performed until 1854), and the early three-act magic opera, *Des Teufels Lustschloss* (1814). Otherwise, it's a sorry tale. *Adrast* (1819–20) was unfinished: *Die Bürgschaft* (1816) got only as far as acts one and two: *Sakuntala* (1820–1) and *Rüdiger* (1823) exist only in incomplete sketches. And so on. Was Schubert incompetent at opera? Was he better off sticking to his hundreds of little songs?

> " ☆ "
>
> ### Curious Fact
>
> Odd, that although there are Schubertiads (see box opposite) – though they actually have nothing to do with his operas – there aren't any Mozartiads or Beethoveniads!

ABOVE Fashionable cafés were the heart of the intellectual, social, and artistic life of the Austrian capital.

1814 The clockwork metronome, an apparatus for sounding a set number of beats per minute, is patented by Johann Maelzel. Its ticking supposedly inspires the theme of the second movement of Beethoven's Eighth Symphony.

1825 Tea roses, so called because they are supposed to smell of tea, are imported to Europe from China for the first time.

1828 Schubert is buried as close as possible to Beethoven, whom he revered and at whose funeral he was a torchbearer, with the slightly grudging epitaph, "Music has here entombed a rich treasure, but still fairer hopes."

BORROWED TIME

It's certainly tempting to accuse Schubert of lacking staying power. Many other works by him survive unfinished, not just operas (and not just *The* "Unfinished" Symphony). If a piece felt right, he would continue until the end; if it took a wrong turn, he simply stopped in his tracks. Too many other ideas needed following up and, suffering the effects of syphilis, he must have been extremely conscious of living on borrowed time.

Schubert wrote German opera when it was not very fashionable in Vienna, so learning from practical experience was difficult. He was good at atmosphere and at mood painting, but not at large-scale dramatic effect. Yet there was massive potential. In his completed works there is increasing concern for dramatically expressive orchestral colors and harmonic relationships, and an integration of set forms intended to expand *Singspiel* into something both more unified and more romantic. He died at just 31. Given another 20 years, who knows what he might have achieved?

ABOVE An oil sketch by Moritz von Schwind, appropriately unfinished, of a Schubertiad.

Schubertiads

Whatever his sexuality – and there is considerable room for debate – Schubert valued close friendships and often gathered with his musical and artistic friends for intimate, convivial evenings, when his latest songs were sung. These gatherings became known as Schubertiads, and the term has been applied to festivals and recitals of his music.

1793 A British navigator, exploring the northwest coast of the U.S., comes across an island of moderate size off British Columbia. It is christened Vancouver Island in his honor.

1812 The Elgin Marbles (not marbles as such, but decorated sculptures from the ruined Parthenon at Athens) are brought to England, starting a controversy that rages to this day.

1815 John Nash rebuilds England's Brighton Pavilion in pseudo-oriental style.

1800~1826

Singspiel on Target
Weber the Romantic

ABOVE Carl Maria von Weber: a life cut short.

Poor old – or young – Carl Maria VON *WEBER (1786–1826) didn't live long, either. But he was a man born to the stage. His father formed the Weber Theater Company and the family spent an itinerant life, performing plays and* Singspiels *all over Bavaria, although protracted stays (mostly occasioned by his mother's illness) in the towns of Hildburghausen and Salzburg enabled Weber to take piano and composition lessons. He wrote his first opera in 1798 at age of 12. We've no idea what it sounded like, because the score was destroyed in a fire.*

Lo and behold, Weber's second opera (composed in 1800) was also lost, apart from a couple of fragments. Yet another followed the next year – we have that one – but then the lad retired to hone

BELOW Grisly scene from *Der Freischütz*: Caspar and Max front it out in the wolf's lair.

Der Vampyr

Heinrich August Marschner's opera *Der Vampyr* (1828) was part of the early Romantic movement. Plays on the vampire theme were popular in France, England, and Germany: the craze quickly spread to the novel, but was slow to reach what should have been its perfect medium – opera. Marschner's example, following the literary model traceable back to Lord Byron, is based in the Scottish castle of Sir Henry Davenant, in the eighteenth century. It proved highly popular for a century, though it had its rivals (see opposite).

1816 The kaleidoscope is invented by Sir David Brewster. Besides the delightful patterns it produces, it has the practical function of enabling designers to realize the effect that can be produced by a symmetrical design.

1824 J.B. Dumas and J.L. Prévost prove that the sperm is essential to fertilization – a sigh of relief is heard from the male population.

1826 Sir Stamford Raffles founds London Zoo, but will be better known for the luxurious colonial hotel named after him in Singapore.

his technique under an influential teacher, the Abbé Vogler, in Vienna. The result was *Silvana* (1810), a mixture of the predictable and the inspired.

It shows, if only sporadically, Weber's ability to respond to nature and to convey emotional tensions in his work.

TO NOTE · NAMES

Early German Romantic opera was cultivated by many fine composers, like **Louis Spohr** *(1784–1859, ten works, including* Jessonda, Der Berggeist, Der Alchymist, *and* Faust*);* **Albert Lortzing** *(1801–51), who specialized in comic operas, most famously* Der Wildschütz *(1842); and* **Ernst Hoffmann** *(known as E.T.A., 1776–1822), whose works include two impressive, serious operas,* Undine *and* Aurora, *and two* buffo-*like works.* **Marschner** *(1795–1861) also wrote other important pieces, though* Hans Heiling *is the only one that ever gets performed these days.*

Other Blood-suckers

Di Palma in 1812 (Naples) and one Mengal in 1826 (Ghent) also got their teeth into the vampire craze. Marschner's only serious rival was, however, Peter Josef von Lindpaintner's *Der Vampyr* (1828). Not quite as tense and terrifying, it still had a real following, which threatened to prevent Marschner's version from reaching the Viennese stage.

ROMANTIC HORROR

At this stage the music was a rather uneasy combination of Germanic, Italian, French, and Viennese elements, and after writing a one-act *Singspiel, Abu Hassan,* Weber concentrated on non-theatrical music for a while. His next opera, the spooky *Der Freischütz* (1821), was a masterpiece, the zenith of the development of *Singspiel*. But *Singspiel* it still was, with spoken dialogue.

Weber's next step was to make a German grand opera without speech. In the heroic-chivalric *Euryanthe* (1823), he chose a mediocre libretto, but wrote a good piece, nevertheless – one that looked to the future of German opera – although his great rival, Louis Spohr's Indian-inspired *Jessonda,* premiered just before *Euryanthe,* and stole its thunder. Weber had yet more libretto problems with his final opera, *Oberon*

(1826), which still includes dialogue, but the music has an elfin brilliance and is beautifully orchestrated. All of which makes Weber's death from tuberculosis, shortly after the first performance of *Oberon* in London, all the more poignant. Like Schubert, Weber's is a tantalizing case of what might have been.

PLOT SLOT

Der Freischütz ("The Freeshooter") goes like this: Max, whom Agathe is due to marry, gets some magic silver bullets that never miss from his friend, Caspar. Caspar has sold himself to the evil spirit Zamiel, who has enchanted the bullets so that the seventh will do *his* work. Wedding/shooting day arrives. Max is successful with six shots, and Prince Ottokar tells him to shoot a dove, which turns out to be Agathe. But she's only fainted – it's Caspar who has been hit and whom Zamiel claims for his own. The Prince banishes Zamiel, but a hermit pleads for mercy, while Max and Agathe get on with the wedding. Simple, really.

1800 British inventor William Murdock uses coal gas to set up experimental gas lighting. Soon cities and better-off homes are lit by flaring gas jets – crime falls and the evening meal becomes the social focus of the day.

1808 At Pompeii, extensive excavations begin on the site buried by volcanic lava from Vesuvius.

1813 Rossini's *L'Italiana in Algeri* is premiered in Venice – Isabella, the new Italian wife chosen for Mustafa, searches for her lover Lindoro, who is Mustafa's slave.

1790~1880
Liberté, Egalité, Fraternité
and Grand Opera

ABOVE *Vive la révolution!*
The people rise up…and sing?

The French Revolution was all about the ending of privilege – at least until Napoleon got ideas above his supposedly egalitarian station. One effect was the flourishing of many small theaters, freed of royalistic tradition. But when Napoleon declared himself Emperor in 1804, grandeur was once again an acceptable aspiration for French opera, just as it had been under old Louis XIV. Operas now became spectacles in which triumphal processions were de rigueur.

Few works written in such mode stood the test of time, though a highly significant composer, admired by Berlioz himself, was the Italian-born *Gaspare* Spontini (1774–1851). His most famous opera, combining French and Italian elements and with a Gluck-like seriousness to it, is *La Vestale* (1805). But it took the Restoration, an injection of new stage technology – gas lighting, and the fancy scenic techniques of Daguerre and Cicéri – and the arrival in Paris in 1824 of one *Gioacchino* Rossini (1792–1868) to create a serious grand opera that really meant something. Oh, and something else – an ingenious librettist who went by the appropriate name of Scribe and brought a little dramatic meat to the form.

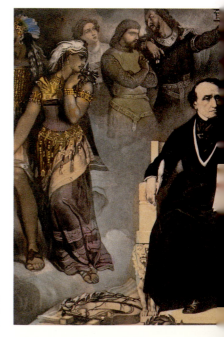

RIGHT Meyerbeer triumphant on a colored postcard, surrounded by the spirits of all the operas he has written.

1816 In a moment of inspiration, French physician René-Théophile-Hyacinthe Laënnec bends a notebook into a cylinder and places one end between a female patient's breasts and the other end to his ear. He has invented the stethoscope.

1823 The opera *Clari, or the Maid of Milan*, is written by Henry R. Bishop and contains the song "Home, Sweet Home."

1825 French law compensates the aristocracy for their losses during the French Revolution – a bit late for those who lost their heads.

TO NOTE NAMES

Composers such as **Gaetano Donizetti** *(see p.62)*, **Charles Gounod** *(1818–93)*, **Giuseppe Verdi** *(see pp.66–9)*, and **Jules Massenet** *(see p.59)*, whose Le roi de Lahore *(1877) was the last such piece of this kind to enjoy great success, also made their own contributions to French grand opera. Turn to p.67 to see how Verdi's* Don Carlos, *the first, five-act version, which was seen at the Paris Opéra in 1867, is perhaps the greatest work written in this tradition.*

A RARE SCRIBE

Eugène Scribe's first piece for the Paris Opéra was for the *opéra comique* composer Daniel Auber's *La muette de Portici* (1828), whose staging involved the small matter of a re-creation of the eruption of Vesuvius as the curtain fell. Easy! Scribe also scribed the words for Rossini's *Guillaume Tell*, an opera famous of repute, but rare of performance. But it was as Giacomo Meyerbeer's librettist that Scribe achieved his greatest success. MEYERBEER (1791–1864) trained in Germany, and had already written Italian operas. Like Rameau and Gluck before him, he brought to Paris a healthy eclecticism. He was good at characterization, taking care that even the minor roles were meticulously drawn. That helped in the subtlety stakes, too.

The Scribe Factory

Eugène Scribe (1791–1861) came from poverty, but got a scholarship and studied law. In the new atmosphere of freedom he became attracted to the lively Parisian theatrical scene. He wrote like the obsessive he was, producing librettos to order; was deft at managing a plot; and could be relied on to give composers what they wanted, and did so – around a hundred times. He became one of the most significant figures of French grand opera, writing for such composers as Rossini, Bellini, Donizetti, Gounod, Halévy, and Verdi.

RIGHT Eugène Scribe at work, a one-man libretto factory, with all his components readily at hand.

1803 In England, the first dahlias – native to Mexico and Central America – are grown.

1821 England's Queen Caroline is offered an annuity of £50,000 to renounce the title of queen and live abroad; she refuses and makes a triumphal entry to London, but is turned away from George IV's coronation a few days before she dies, proving that difficult royal marriages are not a modern phenomenon.

1831 On the streets of New York, the first horse-drawn buses appear.

1800~1870

Brilliant Berlioz

The Orchestration King

ABOVE Hector Berlioz, brilliant but not glittering.

Hector BERLIOZ (1803–69) was one of the most colorful, most passionate, most prodigiously gifted, most outspoken, most skilled, most naive, most bold, most knowledgeable, most caustic, most clumsy, most inspired, most – well, most awesome composers who ever walked this planet. You will deduce that I quite like him. He wrote words with brilliance, using them as effectively for business purposes as for criticism and instruction. He also set music to words with immaculate sensitivity. Listen to his song-cycle Les Nuits d'été, *six songs set to poems by Théophile Gautier, if you want immediate proof.*

But for all that, his operatic career wasn't particularly glittering. When *Benvenuto Cellini* was shown at the Paris Opéra in 1838, it flopped. Then Berlioz had a shot at one of Scribe's librettos, *La nonne sanglante* – "The bloody nun?" Sounds more like a cocktail than an opera – but gave up on it. Gounod eventually wrote the work. Next, Berlioz was rejected for the job of the Opéra's chief conductor, for which he had been strongly recommended. He stalked off to London for nine months, as conductor of Louis Jullien's ill-starred opera company in Drury Lane. Meanwhile, Berlioz's experimental *légende dramatique*, *La damnation de Faust* (1846), had also gone down like a lead balloon. It was never really intended to be staged, though numerous attempts to do so have been made. Such is the fate of the radical.

EPIC AUTOBIOGRAPHY

But then in Weimar, Liszt's patron, Princess Carolyne Sayn-Wittgenstein, gently introduced Berlioz to the idea of writing a vast opera on Virgil's *Aeneid*. The result was *Les Troyens*, composed in a mere two years (1856–8). Even this piece suffered from the demands of practicality: the premiere at the Théâtre-Lyrique in Paris in 1863 was only of its second part, *La prise de Troie*, and both parts were not shown together until well

Harriet Smithson

After he met the beautiful young actress Harriet Smithson in 1827, Berlioz pursued her with a vigor that would probably be deemed illegal today. Eventually they entered into a stormy and fairly bizarre courtship, marrying in 1833. But the relationship petered out, Smithson dying in poverty and misery in 1854.

1840 Nelson's Column is erected in London, to the delight of pigeons in Trafalgar Square.

1846 John C. Horseley designs the first painted Christmas card, little realizing what a phenomenon he will start.

1856 Louis Pasteur gives his name to the process of pasteurization: it will eventually be applied to milk production, but a more vital task is to save wine from turning sour as it ages.

after Berlioz's death, in 1890. Its models included Meyerbeer's works, Gluck's *Orfeo*, Pierre Narcisse Guérin's painting of Aeneas and Dido,

Shakespeare (for whose work – as well as the Irish actress playing Ophelia – Berlioz had been struck with passion "like a thunderbolt"), and his own Romantic vision of Antiquity. But in the end, and in the person of Aeneas, who sacrifices contentment for destiny, *Les Troyens* is autobiography – and a magnificent one at that.

ABOVE Harriet Smithson, B.'s Irish muse, in her inspiring role as Ophelia.

BELOW Aeneas explains to the besotted Dido how it all went horribly wrong at Troy (painting by Guerin). The Trojan Wars inspired Berlioz's *Les Troyens*.

It wasn't, however, Berlioz's operatic swansong. That distinction goes to *Béatrice et Bénédict*, a bubbling two-act piece on Shakespeare's *Much Ado about Nothing*, which was performed in 1862 in Baden-Baden, where Berlioz conducted each summer, to celebrate the opening of a new theater. Berlioz wasn't really a bombast at all.

Berlioz's Writings

Berlioz didn't restrict himself to writing music. His books include a still-used treatise on orchestration and one of the most entertaining musical biographies ever written, his *Memoirs* – ideal for anyone interested in the feverishly imaginative and creatively gifted type that Berlioz was. Then there's *Les Soirées dans l'orchestre*, *Les grotesques de la musique*, and *A travers chants*, collections of sharp, penetrating, and deeply honest criticism. Wagner was not his cup of tea, by any means.

1778 After being organist at a convent since the age of 10, Etienne Méhul is taken to Paris by a rich amateur who recognizes the young boy's talent.

1789 William Bligh and 18 men are cast adrift in a boat in the Pacific after mutinying on the H.M.S. *Bounty*. They eventually reach the Pitcairn Islands.

1791 Haydn composes his "Surprise" Symphony, which shocks audiences with its sudden forte drumbeat in the slow movement.

1780~1800

It's Opéra Comique, Comrades
But Not As We Know It

Before the French Revolution opéra comique *had shown signs of getting serious, but it was still predominantly something light, musically insubstantial, and, despite its satirical and romantic content, aimed to charm the price of a ticket out of anyone. But when the Revolution actually took place, its level of seriousness deepened. So did its grandness. All art was supposed to be for the common person. Although* opéra comique *retained its label, it now strove to improve and astonish, rather than amuse. The presence of spoken text, songs, and melodrama (accompanied spoken recitations) were now what defined its label.*

Sometimes the translation of conventional opera subjects to suit the new mood could be rather farfetched. Luigi Cherubini's *Médée* (1797) radically reinvents the mythological child murderer into a nobly militant feminist, for instance. Many early pieces were also flagrant propaganda, idealizing revolutionary heroes – either through specific reference or through classical (usually Roman) analogy.

Méhul

Etienne-Nicolas Méhul (1763–1817) was Cherubini's most important successor, looking forward to the continuous drama of Weber's *Euryanthe* and even further ahead to Wagner. Key work (for that reason): *Mélidore et Phrosine* (1794). Never staged these days, though.

LEFT Enter the comedians; *opéra comique* returns after the Troubles, but in a darker, more bloodstained mood.

1794 French revolutionary Camille Desmoulins meets his fate at the guillotine none too heroically; two weeks later his wife dies with the courage of a martyr.

1795 In France a logical metric system is developed and adopted, based on the meter, which is to be handily equal to 1/10,000,000 of the distance from the North Pole to the Equator. Because of hostility to the French revolutionaries, the system is slow to catch on.

1797 In Russia Catherine the Great dies – she will be the last monarch to be worthy of the appellation "the Great."

Médée

Here's another *opéra comique* that isn't very funny but fits that genre, simply because it includes spoken dialogue (its libretto is by François-Benoit Hoffman). Its presence in today's limited repertoires is due largely to the interpretation by Maria Callas of its title role in 1952. The opera tells a horrific story of infanticide and spares the audience nothing: revenge and murder sustain the work throughout its three-hour duration. The characterization is deep and the musical impetus relentless, to a degree matched in the field of so-called *opéra comique* only by Bizet in *Carmen*, much later.

TO THE RESCUE

But there was another kind of *opéra comique*, whose plots concerned robbers, tyrants, nasty natural phenomena, chivalric tales, and, following Rousseau, generally heroic human deeds. These pieces had one thing in common. They involved an act of rescue at the very last. Aha! Beethoven's *Fidelio*, the supreme rescue opera, is therefore an *opéra comique*, you will cry. Well, yes, only it was a German one. Confusing, isn't it?

TO NOTE NAMES

Besides Cherubini *and* Méhul, **Jean-François Le Sueur** *(1760–1837) contributed important works to the revolutionary* opéra comique *repertoire of a serious kind. His* La Caverne *(1793) is renowned as his most original effort, though both* Paul et Virginie *(1794) and* Télémaque *(1796) reveal his fingerprints of constant tension and a certain harmonic and melodic harshness.*

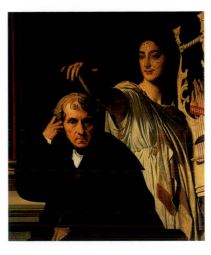

Cherubini

- Luigi Cherubini (1760–1842), Italian-born and a fan of those other famous non-Frenchmen Gluck and Haydn, was the most important of the revolutionary *opéra comique* composers. He added the elements to it that turned it into something serious, influencing Beethoven and the whole German Romantic opera style in the process. His work-list includes nearly 30 operas. Key work besides *Médée: Les deux journées* (1800).

ABOVE Cherubini inspired by his muse in an Ingres painting of 1842.

BELOW Médée, the ultimate bad mother, in a modern production of Cherubini's relentless work.

1805 A German chemist isolates a chemical from laudanum and names it after the Greek work for sleep. Morphine is used to dull pain and induce sleep, though initially its addictive effect is not realized.

1816 Work on the present San Carlo Opera House, Naples, is completed after a mere six months – its audience is said to be the noisiest in Italy.

1825 Sacrilege is made a capital offense in France – does this prompt a rash of religiosity?

1800~1830
Ha, ha, ha! Huh?
Post-revolutionary Opéra Comique

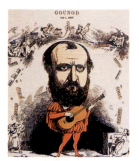

ABOVE Charles Gounod (1818–93), a one-hit wonder with his opera *Faust* (1859).

The revolutionary form of opéra comique *lasted only slightly longer than the new regime's honeymoon period, even though its influence on Germany remained. For a time it was back to the Grétry-like form, as practiced by Adrien* BOIELDIEU *(1775–1834), at least after his somewhat extreme* Béniowski *of 1800, in which the entire cast is saved from a Siberian prison camp. He had a minor rival called Nicolò* ISOUARD *(1775–1818), who came from – of all places – Malta. Gasparo Spontini, he of grand-opera extravagance, also had a tilt at* opéra comique.

But the next noteworthy event was the arrival in Paris of Rossini's *L'Italiana in Algeri* in 1817. Rossini himself (see p.60) followed seven years later. He wrote specifically for Paris and influenced native-grown composers for the next 30 years. Then along came Weber with *Der Freischütz* (1824), which influenced the best of the French-born *opéra comique* bunch of the time, one Ferdinand HÉROLD (1791–1833), who died tragically early. As he himself commented during his last illness, "I was just beginning to understand the stage."

LEFT The victorious Caspar in Weber's seminal work, *Der Freischütz*.

ABOVE Naughty Mephistopheles tempts Gounod's Faust with a vision of fleshly beauty.

1830 In fashion, while ladies' skirts grow shorter, their sleeves become vast and their hats enormous and adorned with ribbons and flowers.

1834 The story of *The Hunchback of Notre Dame* becomes an unlikely bestseller for Victor Hugo.

1848 The first settlers of New Zealand arrive in the South Island at Dunedin – 150 years later, the town still resonates with a Scottish accent.

LEFT Volcanic final scene from *Zampa*, or *The Marble Fiancée* (1831), by Hérold.

The White Lady

La Dame blanche isn't a cocktail in this case, but a superb *opéra comique*, showing how dramatically intense and charming that genre can be, which knocked up over 1,000 performances at the Opéra-Comique by 1862 – one might call it the *Mousetrap* of its time. Orphan Anna's music is particularly beautiful, and the emblematic use of harp arpeggios whenever she appears as the White Lady (okay, I just gave the game away) does not exceed the bounds of taste.

DOUBLE ACT

In mid-century, two guys dominated the scene: our friend the librettist Scribe, who also had a large stake in the grand-opera field, found the right formula; and *his* friend, the composer *Daniel AUBER* (1782–1871), hit on the right sort of light-toned, easy-listening music. Between them the pair created 28 works altogether. Nothing radical happened to *opéra comique* with *Fromental HALÉVY* (1799–1862) and *Adolphe ADAM* (1803–56). Lesser composers made thoroughly trivial pieces, while foreigners like Donizetti made some contributions. So did *Jacques OFFENBACH* (1819–80), who trod a path between *opéra comique* and operetta. So did Charles Gounod, whose *Faust* started life as a *comique*-style piece, complete with dialogue rather than the typically over-lofty recitative – ugh! – that he added later.

Boieldieu

Adrien Boieldieu was by far the most important composer of *opéra comique* in the first quarter of the 1800s. *Le Calife de Bagdad* (1800) led him to take lessons with the wiser, older composer Cherubini. His next opera, *Ma Tante Aurore* (1803), was far more technically accomplished. Boieldieu then went to St. Petersburg, where he wrote *Aline, Reine de Golconde* and eight other comic operas before returning to Paris in 1811. His subsequent works for the Opéra-Comique included *Jean de Paris* (1812) and *La Dame blanche* (1825), to a libretto by (wouldn't you know it?) Scribe. There were also two collaborative works for the Paris Opéra.

1873 Great Italian tenor Enrico Caruso is born in Naples. He will go on to make more than 600 appearances in nearly 40 operas.

1874 Claude Monet's *Impression: soleil levant* gives its name to the art movement that will dominate painting in the years ahead.

1875 The first roller-skating rink opens in London – wheeee!

1870~1880
El Momento de Verdad
Bizet's *Carmen*

ABOVE Jules Massenet (1842–1912), melodious, tuneful – a little bit sweet and dull?

Jules Massenet, Camille Saint-Saëns, and Leo Delibes also had a go at opéra comique, *with only limited success. But then Camille Du Locle, director of Paris's second opera house, the Opéra-Comique, cannily appointed one Georges BIZET (1838–75) to give his institution a kick up the backside. Bizet failed with his one-act piece,* Djamileh, *in 1872, largely because his treatment of a poor libretto was too original. But with* Carmen *(1875), completed just before he died of heart disease, Bizet brought* opéra comique *to new heights – or perhaps one should say new depths.*

C armen is brilliant, though it was coolly received at first. It's a low-life tragedy, based on a novel by Prosper Mérimée, about a fatalistic, sexy cigarette factory worker who is the victim of her own fickleness and destroys her besotted lover, the deserter Escamillo, in the process. It should always be performed with the spoken dialogue and melodrama, rather than with the inferior recitatives composed after Bizet's death by *Ernest GUIRAUD* (1837–92). Bizet knew exactly what he was doing. He doesn't judge; he merely relates, in the most vivid, yet well-balanced terms. The tunes are wonderfully memorable, but so is the profundity of the opera's impact.

Bizet's Other Operas
Bizet didn't just write one opera. Though not as good as *Carmen*, there are a couple of mildly famous operas – *Les Pêcheurs des Perles* (1863) and *La Jolie Fille de Perth* (1867) – and other works. In fact, Bizet regularly received commissions from the Opéra-Comique and the Théâtre Lyrique in Paris. Unfortunately, he died young, at 36, an age when Verdi, for instance, had barely started.

STABBING ON THE STAGE
Anyone accustomed to all the froth that the Opéra-Comique had been showing for decades would have been shocked to see a heroine murdered onstage. So much so that after its premiere, *Carmen* was not seen again in Paris for another eight years. But, once revived, there was no stopping

1876 After spilling some battery acid on his trousers, Alexander Bell yells to his assistant, "Watson, please come here." Watson, on another floor at the end of an electric circuit, hears the instrument speak, and the telephone is born.

1877 Queen Victoria is proclaimed Empress of India.

1878 George Grove begins compiling his *Dictionary of Music and Musicians*, which will grow in scope from a mere four volumes to twenty a century later.

Carmen Jones

This was a 1954 adaptation of Bizet's masterpiece by Oscar Hammerstein, no less, using an all-black cast and set in a World War I army unit. Hammerstein turned the opera into a musical, increasing its popular appeal. The new situation was credible but, despite the great soprano Marilyn Horne playing the title role, Bizet's original score remains a lot richer.

its surge to the top of whatever was the equivalent of the opera charts, where it has since resolutely stayed.

In the process, Bizet had trodden on the toes of the grand-opera camp at the Paris Opéra. Others attempted to follow up his revolutionary work, but its very adventurousness sounded the death-knell for *opéra comique*. Massenet wrote works for both institutions that hardly differed in their approach: spoken dialogue was now reserved for operetta; Emmanuel CHABRIER (1841–94) and Edouard LALO (1823–92) took up the influence of Wagner. And the Opéra-Comique ironically began to get itself a reputation for mounting experimental work.

> **NAMES TO NOTE**
>
> **Saint-Saëns'** most famous opera is Samson et Dalila *(1868, revised in 1877)*, a work of emotional intensity, but there are a dozen others. **Massenet** *(1842–1912)* wrote three works with familiar names – Manon *(1884)*, Werther *(1892)*, and Thaïs *(1894)* out of three dozen operas in all. And of **Delibes'** score or so of operas and operettas, few can name other than Lakmé *(1883)*, though there are some memorable titles – La fille du golfe *(1859)* and L'omelette à la Follembuche *(also 1859)*, for starters.

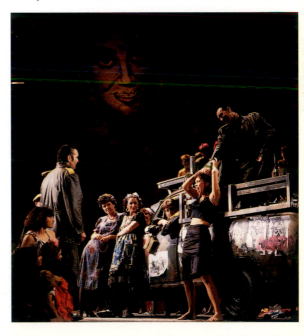

RIGHT Raunchy 1986 version of *Carmen* with Sally Burgess as the feisty heroine.

1815 Venetian Antonio Canova sculpts his "Three Graces" – 180 years later there will be a less than graceful storm about keeping them in a British, rather than an Italian, museum.

1816 Giovanni Paisiello dies in relative poverty, after writing around 100 operas and falling out of favor during the Bourbon Restoration.

1831 Chloroform is discovered simultaneously by an American and a German.

1810~1830

Last of the Great Classicists
Rossini

We've seen how Mozart's operas combine the best elements of opera buffa *and* opera seria *in a single piece, a genre that some call* opera semiseria *(though I'd prefer not to). Thanks to Gluck, et al., opera seria itself had loosened its formulaic shackles and, as a new century dawned, Italian opera composers were increasingly being influenced by French opera – the huge finales of* tragédies lyriques *and the format of the rescue-opera variety of* opéra comique. *Giovanni Paisiello, Ferdinando Paer, and Simone Mayr were among its better-known composers. I won't bother you with the rest – even the keenest of critics have to look them up hastily.*

L ots of radical movements were afoot. In Naples they were even blurring the distinctions between recitative and aria by accompanying the former with full orchestra. But things musical were moving most quickly and most radically in Germany. For a while Italian opera was not very important.

BREAKING THE MOLD
Until, that is, *Gioacchino ROSSINI* (1792–1868) erupted onto the scene with a famous double triumph in Venice, the heroic *Tancredi* (1813) and the comic *L'Italiana in Algeri* (1813). Rossini imposed a new mold on opera. Music for

ABOVE That fiendish fellow, the Barber of Seville; the opera was so popular it inspired sets of colored postcards.

both comedy and tragedy is now written in the same language and forms. The basic unit becomes the scene, rather than the aria. And within the scene there are certain conventional patterns that are almost analogous to sonata form – and equally variable. What's more, ornamentation is now written out, rather than being improvised by the performer, and becomes an integral part of the operatic process, so that arrogant singers aren't able to steal the limelight.

The Lone Ranger

Everyone knows the overture to *Guillaume Tell* (1829; the story's by Schiller) – the one that goes Diddy DUM diddy DUM diddy DUM-DUM-DUM. Well, here's a test. Get your hands on a recording of Rossini's opera overtures; when you reach *William Tell* (it's always there) *do not* indulge in recidivism and think of the cowboy you saw galloping over the range on TV when you were about four. Call me a snob if you like (it's water off a duck's back), but one of the scourges of opera and classical music is the misappropriation of some of the best for purposes unrelated to their original context: soccer songs, airline ads, and so on. *The Lone Ranger* started it off. Thanks for nothing.

ABOVE Rossini quit while he was ahead with *Guillaume Tell* (1839), of overture fame; it was his last work for the stage.

A great composer? Assuredly so. A nineteenth-century composer? Only chronologically. Really, he was the last great classical opera composer.

It helped Rossini's cause that he was an instinctively inventive composer. And these patterns, dramatically sound, provided a framework on which he could quickly organize and discipline his inventiveness in many a bustlingly funny or deeply serious work. He was able to turn instantly from one mood to the other – *Il barbiere di Siviglia* and *Otello*, for instance, were both composed in 1816. He left Italy for Paris in 1824. There he became director of the Théâtre-Italien and wrote pieces in both the French grand-opera and *comique* styles, including for the Paris Opéra, though he stayed only five years.

> TO NOTE   NAMES
>
> *There are around three dozen Rossini operas: if your taste is for the comic variety, then* Il barbiere di Siviglia *is a must; also the one-act* Il Signor Bruschino *(1813), for those with limited time;* Le Comte Ory *(1828) is a French alternative. Of the more serious fare, try* Otello *(1816) for a fascinating comparison with Verdi;* La donna del lago *(1819) to see how he treats Sir Walter Scott's novel; or* Semiramide *(1823, after Voltaire). It's a rich vein. If you have the money, why not let someone else do the choosing, and elect to visit the annual Rossini festival at Pesaro in Italy, where he was born and where they idolize him.*

1825 Italian tenor Giovanni Rubini creates a sensation with his performances in Paris; he will go on to receive today's equivalent of over $30,000 a season in St. Petersburg and will have three Bellini tenor roles composed for him.

1835 *Lucia di Lammermoor*, with its famous "Mad Scene," takes the Neapolitan public by storm.

1839 The first modern bicycle, with a larger rear wheel turned by pedals, is invented by a British blacksmith, Kirkpatrick Macmillan.

1820~1870

Opera Romantica
Bellini, Donizetti, and Mercadante

ABOVE The soprano: fragrant and fragile.

Rossini's format was a convenient model for others, but gradually Italian opera gained something of the Romantic spirit already well established in French and German music. The short-lived Vincenzo BELLINI (1801–35) was the man who opened up these possibilities. Thanks to him and to Gaetano DONIZETTI (1797–1848), opera slowly gave birth to that quintessential figure of the Romantic opera stage, the heroic tenor. Other voices also assumed particular characters – the basso profundo *of minor hermit-like roles, for instance. The soprano was still important, but now composers tended to make the characters pure, distant, fragile, fragrant, and, above all, tragic. Sad endings were the order of the day. Donizetti also created in his* L'elisir d'amore *a new kind of pastoralism. It's the perfect opera of his to start with.*

ABOVE The Bride of Lammermoor: Sir Walter Scott wrote about her, Sir John Millais painted her, and Donizetti put her in an opera.

There was another important composer around at the time, *Saverio MERCADANTE* (1795–1870), who in the 1830s boldly announced a highly significant program for operatic reform. This entailed throwing aside Rossini's structures in favor of more variety, a new

1843 Italian soprano Adelina Patti is born in Madrid; she will become the highest paid singer of her day, with a clause in her contract excusing her from rehearsal.

1853 The largest tree in the world, the aptly named *Wellingtonia gigantea*, is discovered in California.

1865 The first carpet sweeper makes its appearance.

" ★ "

Which is Which?

Many people confuse Bellini and Donizetti. If ever you are faced with them in a blind tasting, here is one simple guideline. Bellini's style is melody-based and has been likened to that of Chopin on the piano; Donizetti, on the other hand, preferred a more muscular music, creating rises and falls in dramatic tension.

ABOVE Sleepy scene from *La sonnambula* by the Sicilian Bellini. It was a huge success when it was written and toured Europe in triumph.

emphasis on drama, carefully gauged orchestral balance (with less bass drum and "a lot less brass band"), and, in short, a far more fluent sense of drama. By 1840, with Bellini dead and Donizetti often working for Paris, Mercadante was the most respected Italian opera composer of all. He pointed the way to Verdi's maturity, but of course we never see any of his operas today, although there are plenty of familiar titles: *Amleto* (1822), *Didone abbandonata* (1823), *Ezio* (1827), *Don Chisciotte* (1830), *Francesca da Rimini* (1830-ish), *La vestale* (1840), *Leonora* (1844), *Violetta* (1853), and something called *I due Figaro* (1829-ish)... So the next time a quiz question asks, "Who, besides Y, wrote the opera X?" – chances are it will be Mr Mercadante. Funny old world, isn't it?

TO NOTE **NAMES**

Donizetti was prolific: 65 operas, not including major revisions (often given new titles). But the most famous, in reverse chronological order, are Don Pasquale *(1843),* La Fille du régiment *(1840),* Lucia di Lammermoor *and* Maria Stuarda *(both 1835) and* L'elisir d'amore *(1832). (Nobody is going to bring up Donizetti's* Gianni di Calais *in idle conversation – at least I hope not.) Only 10 operas in Bellini's case, you'll be happy to hear. The four-star ones are* I Capuleti ed i Montecchi *(1830),* La sonnambula *(1831),* Norma *(1831 again), and* I puritani *(1835).*

1859 Adelina Patti makes her debut in New York under the stage name "Little Florinda"; she is just sixteen.

1861 Daily weather forecasts begin in Britain – 130 years later forecasters are still trying to get them right.

1862 American inventor Richard Gatling has a lot to answer for – he invents the first machine gun and his name lives on in the term "gat" (slang for handgun).

1850~1870

Opera Risorgimenta
Italy after Rossini

ABOVE **Giuseppe Verdi at podium.**

Despite Mercadante, much post-Rossinian Italian opera in the first half of the nineteenth century was a curious affair, peopled by "types" rather than by real, individual characters – and even these were more voice-types than people-types. Today it's considered a bit old-fashioned to compare Italian music with German of the same period. We live in an age when everything – no matter how naïve or coarse – is supposed to be as good as everything else; when the trashy is elevated to the position of art. I don't buy that, and it's just a fact that French and German music, in their very different ways, were miles ahead of Italian at this time, in purely musical terms – richer harmonies, better use of the instrumentarium, and more progressive forms.

The great hope in Italy was *Giuseppe Verdi* (1813–1901), who drew on the confusion of sources around him to forge something personal. (We'll deal with him pp. 66–67.) The faults in everyone else's work weren't, however, entirely their own doing. The censor, mean, reactionary old thing, banned anything that reeked too strongly of the spirit of the Risorgimento (the movement for Italian unification), and so the light-hearted *opera buffa* flourished, restoring the *secco* recitative that Donizetti had jettisoned in his *Don Pasquale* (1843). *Opera semiseria* also came back into fashion. All very retro.

RIGHT **The Devil in all his pomp: Boito's *Mefistofele* at San Francisco, 1989.**

1864 Despite working on the opera for 25 years, Meyerbeer dies before completing *L'Africaine*, which is produced posthumously the following year.

1865 Louis Pasteur saves the French silk industry by curing silkworms of disease.

1868 The first performance of Boito's *Mefistofele* leads to a riot in La Scala between traditionalists and reformers, and finally to the opera's withdrawal on police orders.

TO NOTE · NAMES

There are many minor figures in Italian opera of the period. **Arrigo Boito's** Mefistofele *(1868) is a boldly non-conformist work. Then there were the two* **Ricci** *brothers –* **Luigi** *(1805–59: 30 operas) and* **Federico** *(1809–77: 19 operas);* **Giovanni Pacini** *(1796–1867: I count 86 operas);* **Errico Petrella** *(1813–77: 26 works);* **Carlo Pedrotti** *(1817–93: 19 works);* **Antonio Cagnoni** *(1828–96: 20 operas);* **Filippo Marchetti** *(1831–1902: 7 works);* **Amilcare Ponchielli** *(1834–86: 10 works, including* La Gioconda*);* **Serafino De Ferrari** *(1824–85: 6 works); and* **Emilio Usiglio** *(1841–1910: 7 operas).*

TIME FOR CHANGE

But around 1860, things changed. Conductors – the new musical hero performers – brought operas by Meyerbeer and Gounod to Italy, and Italian composers responded to their influence, diversifying by adopting typical French forms. The librettist/composer *Arrigo BOITO* (1842–1918) wrote a devastating critique of post-Rossinian opera, and, with the composer *Franco FACCIO* (1840–91), produced consciously revolutionary works – *I profughi fiamminghi* (1863) and *Amleto* (1865). Boito's own *Mefistofele* (1868) took the process even further. By 1870 that Italian stock-in-trade, the elaborate cadenza at the end of every slow aria, had disappeared. Thank heavens for that! There's nothing worse than knowing just what to expect and having to wait until it's over before reapplying one's musical and dramatic instincts.

The Risorgimento

Italy had been fragmented since the Vienna Settlement of 1815, drawn up as a result of the Napoleonic Wars. The Risorgimento was the movement that finally resulted in the emergence of a unified kingdom of Italy in 1861. Uprisings by nationalists in 1820 and 1831 were put down, and a Roman republic that was established by Giuseppe Mazzini fell in 1848. But, with the help of the French in a war against Austria, Camillo di Cavour was to lead Piedmont to the unification of Italy within 10 years, and in 1861 Victor Emmanuel II was proclaimed King of all Italy.

RIGHT Garibaldi, hero of the Risorgimento and Victor Emmanuel's right hand man, in his famous red shirt.

1834 Australian ballerina Fanny Elssler makes a sensational debut at the Paris Opéra – she and her sister Therese will go on to wow American audiences.

1842 The triumphant success of *Nabucco* rescues Giuseppe Verdi from the grief that overcame him after the death of his first wife and two children within the space of two years.

1847 Emily Brontë immortalizes the wild beauty of the Yorkshire moors and the destructive power of thwarted love in *Wuthering Heights*.

1830~1870

Italy's National Hero
Viva Verdi!

And Verdi? He wrote his first opera, Oberto, *in 1839, and* Falstaff, *his last and twenty-eighth (not counting revisions) in 1893. It would be surprising if he hadn't done something rather interesting with the form in between. Even his early operas do something different with the post-Rossinian formula. Large, political operas –* Nabucco *(1842),* I Lombardi *(1843),* Attila *(1846), and* La battaglia di Legnano *(1849) – were composed alongside character studies such as* Ernani *(1844),* I due Foscari *(1844),* Giovanna d'Arco *(1845), and the greatest of these early pieces,* Macbeth *(1847).*

In such pieces, ensemble work becomes ever more important. Verdi always insisted on having singers who could really act on the platform. His ability to bring characters to life was shown in *Rigoletto* (1851), considered outrageous at the time for its lack of a real hero and for its onstage depiction of rape. Then came *Il trovatore* (1853), where character study intensifies, followed by the subtle, intimate

ABOVE The maestro Verdi lampooned as an organ grinder; *Don Carlos* is the opera he is "churning out."

Ayeeda!

Don't be tempted to spell *Aida* with a diaeresis: viz. *Aïda*. Despite the pronunciation, this spelling is incorrect in Italian.

La traviata (1853). After which – and who could blame him? – Giuseppe decided, having earned a penny or two, to slow down a bit and take stock of what was happening around him. After the death of his wife, he had shacked up in 1847 with

1854 German watchmaker Heinrich Goebel puts previous inventors in the shade by creating the earliest electric light bulb.

1865 Abraham Lincoln is shot by actor John Wilkes Booth on Good Friday and dies the following day.

1869 The Suez Canal is opened; *Aida* is not, as is commonly supposed, written to celebrate this event, but is premiered at the Cairo Opera House two years later.

the soprano Guiseppina Strepponi, who'd sung roles in his operas and had taken the lead in *Oberto*. In 1853 they settled in Paris (eventually marrying in 1859), where Verdi now spent two years composing his next opera.

Verdi's Life and Times

Verdi was born in Roncole, near Busseto, on 9 or 10 October 1813, to a family of minor landowners, innkeepers, and tradesmen. He began studying at three and his first work was an overture to Rossini's *Il barbiere di Siviglia*, in 1828. After being rejected by the Milan conservatory in 1832, he became a private pupil of Vincenzo Lavigna in Milan, after which he was appointed *maestro di capella* in Busseto. In 1838 his first songs were published in Milan, and he worked on his first complete opera, *Oberto*. Verdi traveled widely in the years 1843–53 and his fees rocketed. He returned to Italy in 1857, his operas of this time reflecting an increasing internationalism. Meanwhile, in 1861 Cavour persuaded him to take a seat in the new Italian parliament, and in 1874 Verdi was elected to the Italian Senate. By the time he died on 27 January 1901, he had earned a fortune and a huge reputation, and Italy saw a genuine outpouring of grief.

FRANCO-ITALIAN ALLIANCE

This work in the grand style for France, *Les vêpres siciliennes*, followed in 1855. But in *Simon Boccanegra* (1857), *Un ballo in maschera* (1859), *La forza del destino* (1862), and, supremely, *Aida* (Cairo, 1871), Verdi gradually forged a new Franco-Italian form of grand opera that breathed joyfully the spirit of newly united Italy. Indeed, in the late 1850s such was the esteem in which nationalists held him that the letters of his surname were adopted as a patriotic acronym. "Viva Verdi!" people would shout, meaning not only long live the composer, but long live Vitorio Emanuele, Re D'Italia. The king must have felt a little angry at the dilution of the tribute. Meanwhile, there had been another piece for Paris – *Don Carlos*, first performed in 1867 – a historical-religious piece that elevated French grand opera to new heights, despite being criticized for what some perceived as Wagnerian influences. And there were still two remarkable masterpieces to come…

LEFT *Don Carlos* in performance at London's Royal Opera House (1996) with Thomas Hampson and José van Damm.

1872 Italian actress Eleanora Duse makes her debut in Verona as Juliet, at the age of just 14. She will go on to triumph across Europe and in New York and rank among the greatest actresses of all time.

1880 Bingo is born from the more interesting-sounding Italian lotto game of *tumbula*.

1883 Post-war British prime minister Clement Attlee and Italian dictator Benito Mussolini are both born.

1870~1900

Verdi and Shakespeare
Otello and *Falstaff*

ABOVE The Swan of Avon sings.

After composing his famous Requiem Mass at the age of 60, Verdi wanted to retire. He didn't need to write in order to eat, after all. But his publishers clearly had other ideas – Verdi was popular and made them money – and in Arrigo Boito found a replacement for his favorite librettist, Francesco Piave, who had died in 1876. The matter of setting Shakespeare's Othello was broached, but at first Verdi would work with Boito only on a revision of Boccanegra. In the end, however, Verdi swallowed the bait, lured not least by Boito's fine libretto. He wrote an equally fine opera – his first for 16 years – given its world premiere in 1887 at La Scala, Milan.

Fine? No, that is an understatement. *Otello* is a great work. It uses traditional forms in a flexible, continuous, entirely new way, at the complete service of the ebbs and flows, the dark intrigue, of the splendid drama it renews. Among its revolutionary, subtle aspects are the integration of declamatory and formal shapes, an uncanny ability to portray mood through the shape of a line, a new refinement of harmony that expresses the minutest inflection of passing emotion and an equally flexible feeling for orchestration. Time now, surely, to retire.

RIGHT Giuseppe Verdi, every inch an Italian hero, in a portrait by Giovanni Boldini (1842–1931).

1886 The celesta, a small keyboard instrument similar to a glockenspiel, is invented by Frenchman Charles Mustel.

1890 The first surgical rubber gloves are worn during an operation in Baltimore.

1901 Verdi, having squeezed into the 20th century, dies, leaving most of his money to a home for elderly musicians that he had founded in Milan.

A DAZZLING FINALE

But no. *Otello* in fact set Verdi thinking again, and although there was a long period of apparent inactivity, he eventually set to work on another Shakespeare play that Boito adapted: the comedy *Falstaff*, based on *The Merry Wives of Windsor* and *King Henry the Fourth*. With subtle insight equal to that shown in *Otello*, Verdi sets the words with a deftness, humor, and, above all, a warming sense of humanity. *Falstaff* (1893) is an ingenious, as well as graceful, operatic bowing out, and another unarguably great work to crown a magnificent career.

ABOVE Program cover for *Falstaff*, showing the old knight in his cups, in authentic Shakespeare style.

ABOVE Placido Domingo as Otello (Royal Opera House, 1985), literally dominated by the hulking figure of Iago.

Shakespeare at the Opera

You might wonder why any composer has the gall to set a playwright as brilliant as Shakespeare. I guess the answer is that genius inspires genius, as well as those who aspire to genius. So here's the low-down (apart from Verdi) on which play inspired which opera:

As You Like It: *Rosalinda* (1744) by Francesco Veracini

The Comedy of Errors: *Gli equivoci* (1786) by Stephen Storace

Hamlet: *Hamlet* (1822) by Giuseppe Mercadante; *Hamlet* (1868) by Ambroise Thomas

Henry IV: *Falstaff* (1838) by Michael Balfe

King Lear: *Lear* (1987) by Aribert Reimann

Macbeth: *Macbeth* by William Davenant

Measure for Measure: *Das Liebesverbot* (1836) by Richard Wagner

A Midsummer Night's Dream: *The Fairy Queen* (1692) by Henry Purcell; *A Midsummer Night's Dream* (1960) by Benjamin Britten

Much Ado about Nothing: *Béatrice et Bénédict* (1862) by Hector Berlioz

Othello: *Otello* (1816) by Gioacchino Rossini

Romeo and Juliet: *I Capuleti ed i Montecchi* (1830) by Gaetano Donizetti

The Tempest: *The Tempest* by William Davenant

Timon of Athens: *Timon of Athens* (1991) by Stephen Oliver

1884 Pietro Mascagni wins a contest for new operas run by Italian music publisher Edoardo Sonzogno. The winning entry – none other than *Cavalleria rusticana* – will establish the reputations of both men.

1891 The zipper is invented by W.L. Judson, though for some reason it doesn't catch on until 1919.

1892 English contralto singer Clara Butt sings the title role of Gluck's *Orfeo* at the Lyceum with notable success, but then opts to pursue a career on the concert platform.

1880~1900

The Path to Verismo
Cav, *Pag*, and Puccini

ABOVE Ruggero Leoncavallo.

The music of Wagner (see pp. 76–81) had far-reaching influence throughout Europe, spreading its tentacles to France, Italy, even England. Mostly that influence didn't take the form of imitating Wagner's leitmotiv technique, but rather the concept of the act (rather than the scene) as the prime musical unit, with the orchestra playing a more significant role than hitherto. Alfredo Catalani's La Wally *(1892) and the young Giacomo Puccini's* Le villi *(1884) had shown hints of what might lie ahead for Italian opera.*

Then, in 1890, *Pietro* MASCAGNI (1863–1945) burst on the scene with his one-act *Cavalleria rusticana*. It was labelled an opera in the *verismo*, or realistic, style, analogous to the French writer Emile Zola's novels of life in the gutter. In fact, it is a bit of a stylistic mishmash. There's Wagnerian weight in the incident and interplay; the harmonies are Gallic; but the solo vocal writing is in the most Italianate, ornate tradition. The words are conversational rather than versified. And the subject is simple: Human Passion, with a capital H and a capital P.

Cavalleria rusticana opened the floodgates. Next came Ruggero Leoncavallo's two-act *Pagliacci* (1892, and long paired with the source of its inspiration in the operatic theater)

RIGHT Scene from *Cavalleria rusticana*, an everyday story of country folk, with added arias.

1896 A new lecture room at Harvard University has a minor defect – the lecturer can't be heard – so the science of architectural acoustics is discovered by Wallace Clement.

1898 Arturo Toscanini becomes artistic director at La Scala, on which he will stamp his inimitable style for the next 10 years.

1900 As the new century is ushered in, the Cake Walk becomes the dance to celebrate by.

Zola (1840–1902)

All the low-life stuff of *verismo* opera has a parallel in the work of the French novelist Emile Zola. His principal work was the 20-novel cycle *Les Rougon-Macquart*, which he called "the natural and social history of a family under the Second Empire." The work focuses on people's less noble instincts, on vice and misery, greed and poverty. It's all dark stuff, with individual novels based on self-contained circumstances. *Germinal*, for instance, is set in a mining community; *La Terre* in a farming community; *L'Assommoir* in the taverns, *La Débâcle* in war. But Zola's writing (even in translation) is wonderfully lyrical, ennobling as it were the ordinary in their extraordinary, heightened emotional condition. It all goes to prove that no art-form is an island.

and *Zazà* (1900); Francesco Cilea's *L'arlesiana* (1897) and *Adriana Lecouvreur* (1902); Umberto Giordano's *Andrea Chénier* (1896) and *Fedora* (1898); and Mascagni's own *Iris* (1898).

In their day, these pieces had considerable impact and many are still seen regularly. But they are really only supporting acts for the composer who brought *verismo* to its fullest, most passionate, most sentimental, and most popular flowering: Giacomo Puccini, who still dominates the repertoire of most of the major opera houses today. Ah well, better get on to him, I suppose.

Cav and Pag

Like bread and butter, and money and corruption – *Cav* and *Pag* are inseparable: both examples of *verismo* opera, both tales of low life and exaggerated (hardly realistic) emotions. *Pagliacci* (never prefix the title with the Italian definite article "I") is about a group of strolling players and uses the device of the play within the play, ending in a double murder that takes place on the strollers' stage – twice removed, as it were, from the real audience. *Cavalleria rusticana* is set in a Sicilian village where a rustic code of honor holds sway. Again it ends in death, this time as a result of a partner-swap by the heroine-figure, Santuzza. And there's another *Cav* (1907), by one Domenico Monleone.

LEFT Pietro Mascagni, the other half of the *Cav* and *Pag* team; he was responsible for *Cav*.

1858 Giacomo Puccini is born in Lucca, Italy. With four immediate paternal ancestors as opera composers, his fate might be thought to be pre-destined; their legacy certainly wins him a subsidy to study at Milan.

1861 Australian soprano Nellie Melba, who will be remembered as much for the ice-cream dessert and toast named after her as for her great London triumphs, is born near Melbourne.

1865 Lewis Carroll ventures into Wonderland for the first time. His original manuscript will be sold to an American buyer for £15,400 in 1928.

1850~1900

Puccini and the Kleenex Factor
The Crying Game

ABOVE Giacomo Puccini, the man who made housemaids weep.

Why so reluctant? Because to do full justice to Puccini would take a lot more space than there is. But also because the snob inside me resents his popularity, achieved by trading on sentimentality. And because his operas keep so many other operas off the stage. Their number can be gauged by looking at the balance of this book. If the space devoted to each composer reflected the regularity of their performances, Puccini would probably take up at least a quarter all by himself.

Giacomo PUCCINI (1858–1924) created a winning operatic formula, focusing on intense human emotions within exotic localities, which were often reflected in the music. Examples? The Wild West for *La fanciulla del West* (1910); an imaginary China for *Turandot* (1926); a relatively real Japan for *Madama Butterfly* (1904); a Parisian garret and café for *La Bohème* (1896). Into such settings Puccini places characters who are, frankly, larger than life. There is the starving, consumption-ridden Mimi in *La Bohème*; the pathetic Butterfly, seduced and deserted by an American lieutenant; Tosca, who hurls herself over the battlements when her lover is shot – all women, all victims of desperate love, and all end up dead. The principal men are either villains (if they are baritones) or lovers (if they are tenors), but whether they live or die they are really catalysts in the final demise of the diva.

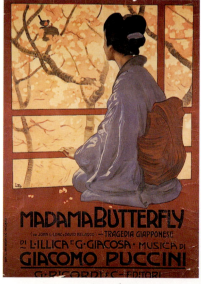

ABOVE Cover of the musical score of *Madama Butterfly*; poor deluded Butterfly waits for the love-rat Pinkerton to return.

1877 W.S. Gilbert's inventive wit and Arthur Sullivan's melodic brilliance are combined for the first time in *The Sorcerer*, which runs for 175 nights.

1883 British inventor Hiram Maxim invents the fully automatic machine gun, giving rise to the jingle, "Whatever happens, we have got/The Maxim gun, and they have not!"

1892 Pineapple is canned for the first time, but this doesn't significantly lower its Vitamin C content.

WEEP YOUR HEART OUT

Are there any cheerful Puccini operas, I hear you ask? Well, yes. *Turandot* ends happily enough, when the princess realizes that her strange suitor is a prince and immediately decides he'll do. But you don't go to a Puccini opera to be cheered up, even when the ending *is* happy. You go to weep your heart out. And, of course, to marvel at the lovely arias.

These are often plucked from their original context and used to fill up many a disc of operatic favorites, but believe me, that's not the best way to hear them. For one thing, Puccini's operas are carefully constructed entities, with motives used to knit the work together and signal certain significant moments. For another, Puccini's arias don't tend to come in neat little packages with their ends tied up like sausages, but as part of a continuous musical fabric. The famous "Nessun dorma," the aria that Luciano Pavarotti sang as the theme song for the 1990 World Cup in Italy, is a good example. It had to be discreetly snipped, as it were. But I don't want to be too snobbish about this. Better a tempting morsel than none at all.

Mrs. Puccini

Puccini lived with Elvira Gemignani from 1886, and she bore him a son before they married in 1904. But Puccini was a bit of a rascal, and Elvira became jealous and bitter to the point of paranoia. She even drove a servant, whom she suspected of an illicit liaison with her husband, to suicide. Amazingly there was a reconciliation, though the relationship was always difficult. A bit of an opera plot in itself?

Tenor morsels

Puccini's repertoire is full of choice morsels for a dramatical-lyrical tenor with power, drama and a ringing high C to relish and show off his talents. "Nessun dorma" is the quintessential example, though it's a pity more people don't hear it in context in *Turandot*, as a song of vigil that might result in the singer's own death, and musically part of a seamless sequence. Another famous tenor number is "Che gelida manina" from *La Bohème*, which most people know as "Your tiny hand is frozen" – opera never was translated into English with an overkill of skill. (Most common line: "Oh, I am so unhappy!") Other winning numbers: "E lucevan le stelle" and "Recondita armonia" from *Tosca*, and "Donna non vidi mai" from *Manon Lescaut*. Contrary to popular view, neither "O sole mio" nor "My Way" are hits by Puccini, though I can see the connection.

BELOW Placido Domingo as Cavaradossi and Della Jones as the eponymous heroine in *Tosca*, a tale of lust, corruption, death, and battlements.

1898 Actor and singer Paul Robeson is born in Princeton. He will give up a career as an attorney at the American bar to take up a stage career.

1903 Verdi's tragic opera in four acts, *Ernani*, becomes the first opera to be recorded.

1909 The "Plastic Age" hits an unsuspecting world, with the first commercial manufacture of Bakelite, named after its inventor, Leo Hendrik Baekeland.

1850~1924

Good Stories, Great Tunes
Puccini's Secrets of Success

Puccini's single most impressive quality was his ability to write a good tune, and, moreover, a tune that grows from, rather than being imposed upon, the dramatic and emotional situation of the character who sings it. This subtle difference is important. His arias often begin slowly, with the orchestra playing the main theme and the voice coming in reflectively with repeated notes, as if a touch distracted from the real world. Then he builds the intensity to its glorious vocal fulfillment. Like most composers, Puccini is always at his best when he is at his saddest, his most poignant. The orchestral writing can be rich, like Richard Strauss, or ultra-refined and spare, like Debussy. But the orchestra is always large, and he uses it well.

ABOVE Sob your heart out with Puccini.

Then there is Puccini's unerring dramatic sense. Every Puccini opera has at least one spectacular, visually arresting scene. He has an instinctive understanding of dramatic movement – the action, at the right moments, stands still – and he knows the power of quiet music, even of silences. What's more, his plots get to the point quickly, without distracting sub-plots or over-complex relationships, even if that means some severe editing of Puccini's literary model.

" ★ "

Turandot's Ending

Confession time: Puccini died of throat cancer before he could finish *Turandot*. His own music stops in the middle of the final act. The work was completed by Franco Alfano. He used Puccini's sketches, and although some claim to hear a distinction between the two styles, in the theater the work moves magnificently to its conclusion.

LEFT The ice-princess Turandot wreaks vengeance for a slight on her family.

1913 Richard Nixon is born; there will be a lot of water under the gate before his career comes to a slushy end.

1920 By experimenting on dogs, American pathologist George Hoyt Whipple discovers that liver is the best food for correcting anemia.

1924 Puccini dies, leaving his ice-princess Turandot suspended in frozen limbo.

WORKS AND PLOTS

La Bohème: Girl dies of consumption in Parisian garret after relationship with impecunious poet breaks up.
Tosca: Evil police chief tortures Republican hero so that heroine will submit to his advances, then arranges mock-execution of hero, which turns out to be real. Heroine throws herself off ramparts.
Madama Butterfly: Gullible young Japanese girl marries cynical American naval officer. He goes back home; she waits. He returns with new wife; she kills herself.
Turandot: Chinese ice-princess proclaims she'll only marry the person who can solve three riddles. Stranger solves them, then turns out to be a prince and marries the now-melted ice-princess.
La fanciulla del West: Self-empowered innkeeper rescues the disguised bandit she's fallen in love with from hanging.

ABOVE *La Bohème*: never a dry eye in the house.

The Other Turandot

Just as Leoncavallo wrote another *La Bohème* (1897), so Ferruccio Busoni (1866–1924) wrote another *Turandot* (1917), although it isn't regarded as his best opera. Busoni was an intellectual polymath, antipathetic toward Wagner, but adoring of Bach, Liszt, and Mozart, and sympathetic to what Schoenberg was trying to achieve (see pp.96–7). More successful than *Turandot* was his brilliant one-act *Arlecchino* (also 1917). But his undoubted masterpiece was *Doktor Faust*, based on sixteenth-century puppet plays and left unfinished when he died. It is now regarded as one of the most significant achievements of the early part of the twentieth century, though you won't find many performances around.

Such a giant talent might well have marked a climactic end-of-the-road for the path of *verismo*. But it was not to be. Other composers who followed in the tradition of Puccini included *Riccardo* ZANDONAI (1883–1944), *Franco* ALFANO (1876–1954, who finished *Turandot* after Puccini's death), and *Italo* MONTEMEZZI (1875–1952). And the most notable of several late practitioners of the style is *Gian Carlo* MENOTTI (b. 1911, see p.113).

1823 In Great Britain the mackintosh (or raincoat) takes its name from the waterproof fabric invented by Scottish chemist Charles Macintosh.

1834 American inventor Cyrus Hall McCormick patents the reaping machine.

1855 Wagner conducts a series of orchestral concerts in London. Queen Victoria and Prince Albert are very enthusiastic.

1820~1890
Life, the Universe, and...
Wagner's Early Operas

ABOVE Richard Wagner, a keen conductor.

We've been neglecting German opera since Weber. High time now for a healthy dose. The next major operatic star in the German firmament was Richard WAGNER (1813–83), who brought to fruition the vision that Weber could only dream of. Wagner, never one to do anything by half-measures, took the complete range of Romantic influences – literary, philosophical (Schopenhauer and Nietzsche in particular), theatrical, political, you name it – and, adding a large measure of determination, ego, and talent, forged a kind of opera intended to synthesize the constituent arts that until then had jostled for position in the operatic hierarchy.

BELOW Commerce coupled with high art: here is Tannhaüser, trying really hard to escape from the Mount of Venus.

For Wagner, opera was religion, its sacred rituals to be observed to the last detail. He wrote his own librettos, designed his own scenery, and directed his own productions. His work even spawned a new kind of singing voice, the *Heldensopran* and *Heldentenor* (heroic soprano and tenor). And one idea ran through all of his operas. From the Weber-influenced *Die Feen* (1834) to his final triumph, *Parsifal* (1882), Wagner pursued the dramatic ideal of redemption through love.

THE OPERA AS SYMPHONY
Wagner used motifs – tiny musical ideas – to unify *Das Liebesverbot* (1836), modeled on Shakespeare's *Measure for Measure* and showing influences from all over the place

1860 Artur Schopenhauer, pessimist philosopher, dies. Violent, lonely, friendless, and distrustful (though he did have a poodle called Atma, or "world soul"), his philosophy of the supremacy of the Will is music to the Wagnerian ear.

1872 Philosopher Friedrich Nietzsche, inventor of the Übermensch (super being) and Schopenhauer's disciple, dedicates his first book, *Die Geburt der Tragödie* (*The Birth of Tragedy*) to Wagner. They disagree four years later when Nietzsche finds *Parsifal* "too Christian."

1886 King Ludwig II of Bavaria, Wagner groupie, and builder of unnecessary palaces, is declared insane.

Controversy

Wagner was a bit of a political animal, and got caught up in the 1849 uprising in Dresden that followed the February Revolution in Paris. He was forced to flee to Switzerland. If he'd been caught, he would probably have been executed. He also wrote quite a lot of prose, including an autobiography (of course), treatises, short stories, and essays, one of which – directed against Meyerbeer – gave Wagner the reputation of being an anti-Semite. He'd incautiously used the words "Hebrew flavor" as a criticism. The reputation stuck, and it wasn't helped by Hitler's declared devotion to Wagner's music. There's still argument about this, not least between surviving members of his own family.

ABOVE At home with the Wagners; a scene of high-toned *Gemütlichkeit* with Wagner, Cosima Liszt, his future wife, and Franz Liszt, his future father-in-law.

(Italy and France, as well as Germany). But he was still a long way from the fully fledged leitmotiv techniques of his mature operas. It's in *Der fliegende Holländer* (1843) that the most obviously radical changes in style are seen. Wagner thought of it as his debut as a poet, and although once again it was based again on a Weber-like German Romanticism, it achieved a continuity and reached deeper emotional depths. Music and drama just flow. In *Tannhäuser* (1845, but twice revised and never considered finished) and in *Lohengrin* (1850) Wagner took the process a bit further. Now he was aiming at making an opera into something more like a symphony. And, by the way, the orchestration's marvelous. Definitely to be played loudly.

Leitmotiv

The term leitmotiv was applied to Wagner by his friend Hans von Wolzogen in 1878. It describes motifs that can be melodic, harmonic, or rhythmic, denoting particular characters, situations, mood, or psychological elements. By their nature they are not rigid, but transform and interreact, according to the situation.

1852 In America, sparrows are imported from Germany to act as a deterrent to caterpillars.

1856 Friedrich Bechstein founds his piano-making firm in Berlin.

1861 Prince Consort Albert dies of typhoid; he has popularized the Christmas tree and is commemorated in a typically Victorian monument opposite the Royal Albert Hall.

1850~1880

The Ring...and the Rest

Wagner's Music Dramas

ABOVE Ludwig II of Bavaria.

What the difference is between an opera and a music drama is a matter of opinion, but I guess Wagner would say that opera becomes music drama when all its constituent parts become fully integrated. At any rate, Wagner's Der Ring des Nibelungen, Tristan und Isolde, Die Meistersinger von Nürnberg, *and* Parsifal *all fall into the music drama category. The first,* Der Ring, *itself consists of four works, and thus stands as the most epic opera ever (but Karlheinz Stockhausen is working on that, see pp.118–19). In order of performance, its constituent pieces are* Das Rheingold *(1854, and a mere one-act bagatelle of an introduction),* Die Walküre *(1856),* Siegfried *(1871), and* Götterdämmerung *(1874).*

In *Der Ring*, the idea of the leitmotiv really takes off. All the leitmotivs in *Der Ring* (first performed as an entity in 1876 at Wagner's new Bayreuth Festival Theater) have their seed in a single note – a low E-flat. From that are derived the ascending pitches of the harmonic series, pitches that get closer together as they get higher. The leitmotivs become ever more complex and precisely defined in meaning: colliding, combining, and reacting with each other to produce new associations. It all sounds so deep, doesn't it? Well, it is. Very deep. A conscious attempt to manipulate the subconscious, no less. I wish I could make it sound fun, but in Wagner's case you have to dig quite hard before you reap your rewards. Believe me, it's worth it – the

ABOVE Lohengrin arrives at Anversa in a picture from Neuschwanstein, mad King Ludwig II's Bavarian *schloss*.

1863 German chemist Adolf von Baeyer discovers barbituric acid, which will be used to make sleeping pills. An apocryphal tale says that he named it after his current girlfriend, Barbara.

1870 Wagner finally marries Liszt's daughter, Cosima, and ex-wife of Hans von Bülow, music director at Munich, after she has already borne him two daughters.

sound is amazing, and even *Der Ring* has some comic moments if you look hard enough, and if your sense of humor is – how to say this? – of Teutonic bent.

Oh, the story … well, it's about this golden ring, and curses and betrayal, and sacrifices and that sort of thing. Go and find out for yourself!

ABOVE The monstrous regiment…Everybody's idea of the ideal Valkyries.

BELOW Modern Walküre in the Berlin Stadtsoper's 1993 *Ring* cycle.

PLOT SLOT

Wagner started *Der Ring* in 1848, basing his text on the medieval *Edda* and *Nibelungenlied* to link the tragedy of Siegfried's death with the myths of the German gods. His subject was modest: the beginning and end of the world. This was to become *Götterdämmerung*. When Wagner's initial attempts to write music for it failed, he wrote another text, *Der junge Siegfried* (later just plain *Siegfried*), to set events in context. More second thoughts, then back to the drawing board to put *Siegfried* into its own context – *Die Walküre*. Then – well, you've guessed it. Once he had the words for *Das Rheingold*, he could write music that worked.

Best and Worst

Nastiest character: Alberich.
Most impressive character: Brünnhilde.
Most dashing character: Siegfried.
Most bizarre relationship: that between the twins Siegmund and Sieglinde.
Sex symbols: I disapprove, but the Rhinemaidens are supposed to be pretty voluptuous.

1857 Gustave Flaubert scandalizes French society with his powerful tragedy of *Madame Bovary*, which is condemned as immoral and its author prosecuted.

1861 *Tannhäuser* is whistled off the stage of the Paris Opéra, chiefly by members of the Jockey Club.

1866 "Black Friday" occurs on the London Stock Exchange; 121 years later "Black Monday" will occur, followed in 1997 by "Brown Tuesday"…

1850~1880

Love and Death

Die Meistersinger, *Tristan*, and *Parsifal*

ABOVE The Holy Grail, Wagner's Arthurian icon.

That leaves only the small matter of Tristan und Isolde, Die Meistersinger, *and* Parsifal. *These three pieces are easy to tell apart.* Tristan *is about Death and Love.* Die Meistersinger *is about Art and Love.* Parsifal *is about Religion and Love. None lasts more than a single evening, but they're all long, and they're shattering experiences. Even* Die Meistersinger *(1867), ostensibly a comedy, has a serious message. Tradition, it pronounces, must be preserved, not overthrown. But tradition also needs constantly to renew itself in order to be preserved.*

Tristan, finished in 1859, is *the* opera. The basic story is simple enough: Tristan (based on the hero of Celtic legend) and Isolde (whom Tristan is taking to be King Mark's bride) meet and then they die. Well, there's a little more to it than that. The music is more than touching – it is voluptuous, engulfing, everything that a good love affair should be (including the hard work). It's also Wagner at his most revolutionary, and that means a lot. In *Tristan*, the whole of Western music finds itself at a crossroads. The concept of key, or tonality – under threat really ever since Beethoven – is compromised by free, chromatic, expressive harmony. There's no longer a point of departure and arrival but a continuous flux, or rather a continuous fluctuation of degrees of suspense. Nowhere to rest, to resolve….

After *Tristan*, Western music was never quite the same. The old classical rules were suddenly irrelevant. Wagner asked some uncomfortable questions – just how deep into the psyche can music penetrate when it's allowed to? – which continue to be posed, for the point of *Tristan*'s music is precisely the freedom of expression that it unleashed.

PLOT SLOT

Wagner restores the concept of set numbers to *Die Meistersinger* without destroying its continuity. The part of the endearing, self-denying Hans Sachs is a gem. Beckmesser, the town clerk, is the resentful comic critic-figure. And Walther is the dashing young hero with a mysterious new spin on the Guild of Mastersingers' Rules of Good Song. In other words, he's Wagner. That's obvious. He gets the prize *and* the girl.

1873 Germany adopts the mark as its unit of currency.

1878 The microphone is invented by English inventor David Hughes. He will leave a large fortune to London hospitals when he dies.

1879 Thomas Edison's first light bulb burns continuously for 40 hours; he then illuminates an entire street before a crowd of 3,000.

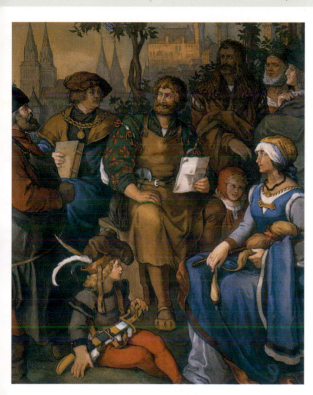

The Holy Grail

Parsifal has Arthurian connections. Parsifal is in fact Sir Percival, Knight of the Round Table, who, according to Sir Thomas Malory, won sight of the Holy Grail. Wagner's version draws on Wolfram von Eschenbach's thirteenth-century account. Many people wonder what exactly the Holy Grail was. Can you eat it? No, and it's probably sacrilegious to drink out of it, for it's the cup used by Christ at the Last Supper. Wagner's opera, heavily symbolic, replete with Holy Spear and Wounded Swan, is all about redemption and the true and pure nature of love.

LEFT Scenes from the *Die Meistersinger von Nürnberg* decorating the walls of Neuschwanstein Castle.

RELIGION AND LOVE

Does *Parsifal*, Wagner's last opera, finished in 1882, go any further? In a way, yes. Like *Der Ring*, its sources are mythology, principally the legend of the Holy Grail (no snickering references to Monty Python). Kundry is temptress, but also the agent through which Parsifal redeems himself. He in turn is able to effect her redemption. Each act represents Parsifal's awakening pity at a particular stage recognized for what it is and then directed outward. It is Wagner's most difficult work, monumental and static, ritualistic, and of course psychologically highly complex. It's the opera to tackle last of all, once the Wagner bug has bitten deep. But don't, as I once did, have any alcohol before or during *Parsifal*. Slow it may initially seem, but you need to absorb yourself entirely in this music in order to come to an understanding of it.

1809 Nikolai Gogol, the Russian author who will specialize in satire that evokes "laughter through tears" is born in Poltava.

1830 Stiff collars become an essential part of a gentleman's attire.

1831 The Russian theosophist Helena Blavatsky is born – her psychic powers will be widely acclaimed, but will not stand up to investigation by the Society for Psychical Research.

1800~1860
The Birth of Russian Opera
Glinka

ABOVE Russian folklore, Glinka's inspiration.

Anybody might think from all that's gone before that opera didn't exist outside Britain, France, Italy, and Germany. Not true. Many other countries, responding to the demands of artistic fashion, had been importing the stuff almost since it was invented. Then in due course they began to make their own. A bit like opening a vodka factory in the North of England, you might think, except that the vodka eventually took on local characteristics.

Since I've mentioned vodka, we may as well start with Russia. There, thanks to Peter the Great and his building of St. Petersburg as a "window on the West," Italian and French operas were often staged in the eighteenth century. The first opera actually by a Russian was Dementy

Glinka's Life and Times
Mikhail Glinka had the good fortune to be born on a Russian country estate, where he heard much folk music, as well as the cultivated stuff that his rich uncle's house orchestra performed. He went to St. Petersburg to study the piano with the Irish composer John Field, joined the civil service, but left on health grounds, going to Italy instead. Good move. There he met Donizetti and Bellini, after which it was off to Berlin, where he studied with the famous teacher Siegfried Dehn. Back in Russia he set about composing *Ivan Susanin* on the subject of the Polish invasion of 1613. After finishing *Ruslan and Ludmila*, this inveterate traveler went first to Paris, then to Spain – which just goes to show that you don't have to be a xenophobe to be a nationalist artist. Poor Glinka wasn't the healthiest of creatures, but perhaps it's fitting that he should have died in Berlin, during further studies with Dehn.

1835 Dry ice is produced by allowing solid carbon dioxide to evaporate, reaching a temperature as low as -110°C – lower than any temperature recorded on the Earth's surface, even in Antarctica.

1843 It is estimated that Cuba has a slave population amounting to 436,000.

1854 Tennyson's "The Charge of the Light Brigade" celebrates the Battle of Balaclava, in which the soldiers' balaclava helmets failed to save them from the bitter weather or the ill-timed engagement.

Zorin's *Rebirth* of 1777, followed by Mikhail Sokolovsky's comic opera *The Miller-Magician, Cheat and Matchmaker* in 1779. This latter work, depicting Russian peasant life in a mixture of speech and songs, was to be a model for many others. But early on there was also a penchant for historical operas and fairy-tale settings that was no less indicative of future directions.

BELOW Mikhail Glinka in the throes of creating his folk-inspired opera, *Ruslan and Ludmila*.

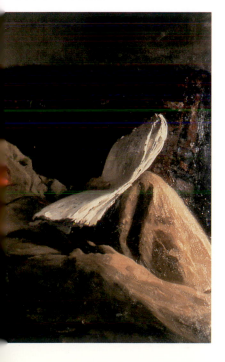

SLAVIC STIMULUS

The first Russian opera composer of real international stature – the man who made Russian music Russian – was *Mikhail* GLINKA (1804–57), largely self-taught but with a real instinct for orchestration. Glinka wrote two operas: a historic epic, *Ivan Susanin* (1836), and a fantasy-comedy, *Ruslan and Ludmila* (1842), based on a poem by Alexander Pushkin. As one might expect, Glinka's operatic style did not come from nowhere – it was strongly influenced by the Italian models of Bellini and Donizetti. But it was still highly individual and very, very Russian. *Ivan Susanin* (also known as *A Life for the Tsar*) is the more Italian of the two, but still contains folkish elements, such as five-beat bars. *Ruslan* introduces the oriental-exotic elements to Russian music that were to be part of it up to, and including, Stravinsky in the next century.

Pushkin at the Opera

Glinka wasn't the only one to be inspired by Pushkin, whose writings are so rich in character and broad in scope, his language so innately musical, that scarcely a Russian composer worth his salt has avoided setting him. He grasped equally well the sophisticated, the peasant, and the mythological sides of Russianness, so that composers had the richest of dramatic veins to mine. Dargomïzhsky's *The Stone Guest* (1872), Mussorgsky's *Boris Godunov* (1874), Rimsky-Korsakov's *Mozart and Salieri* (1897), *Tsar Saltan* (1900), and *The Golden Cockerel* (1907), Tchaikovksy's *Queen of Spades* (1890), *Mazeppa* (1883), and *Yevgeny Onegin* (1878), Rachmaninov's *Aleko* (1892, based on "The Gypsies"), Stravinsky's *Mavra* (1922, on "The Little House at Kolomna")...not a bad little list, is it?

1849 Amelia Bloomer champions the right of women to wear trousers, which subsequently take her name.

1867 Russia sells Alaska to the United States for $7,200,000; five years later, gold is discovered.

1871 Rasputin, who will be the notorious black sheep of Russian court life for his magnetic power over the Tsarina and un-monkish sex life, is born in Tobolsk province.

1840~1890
Verismo Russian-style
Mussorgsky and Borodin

ABOVE Modest Mussorgsky, brought down by drink.

Glinka's two operas each spawned successors in their respective molds. Ivan Susanin's successors included works like Alexander Borodin's Prince Igor *(1890) and Modest Mussorgsky's* Boris Godunov *(1874), the massive work that is generally regarded as Russia's finest contribution to nineteenth-century opera.* Ruslan and Ludmila *gave rise to fantastic operas by Nikolai Rimsky-Korsakov (see pp. 86–87) and others.*

L ater in the century another, contrasting movement developed, called "musical realism." Its music was based on the first principles of opera, that the vocal line should follow the inflections of speech – "melodic recitative" was the term coined. One of the most significant works written in this way was Alexander Dargomïzhsky's *The Stone Guest* (1872), a setting of a long poem by Pushkin. A little earlier, in 1868, the notoriously alcoholic *MUSSORGSKY* (1839–81) had had a try at the same sort of style in his setting of Nikolai Gogol's *The Marriage*, but he didn't finish the piece. It was significant because it includes the first use of leitmotiv in Russian opera. But musical-realist operas risked being a bit monotonous, so in *Boris Godunov* (completed in 1869, and the only opera he *did* finish), Mussorgsky combined a melodic recitative style with something more like Glinka's lyricism. That's why it works so well.

Mussorgsky
Like Glinka, Mussorgsky heard much folk music in childhood and became a civil servant. One might imagine a neatly dressed gentleman fervently scribbling a few pages more of opera on his coffee breaks. In fact, he was a disheveled, lazy person, haunted by the alcoholism that finally killed him. But his artistic vision was clear, and his brand of musical realism aimed at – and achieved – an immediate, vivid, and wholly Russian effect.

LEFT Designs for Borodin's *Prince Igor,* for the 1914 Bolshoy production.

1873 Under the catchy name of *Sphairistike*, the modern game of lawn tennis is introduced to Britain at a garden party.

1881 Modest Mussorgsky dies an early death hastened by alcoholism.

1897 Queen Victoria notches up her Diamond Jubilee.

Borodin

Alexander Borodin was also a part-time composer. In real life he was a professor of chemistry, and he founded a School of Medicine for Women; an upright sort of man compared with old Mussorgsky, he became a member of The Five (with Cui, Mussorgsky, Rimsky, and Balakirev himself, see p.89) when he met Balakirev in his late twenties. But his busy main career limited his output – he'd joke about being able to write only when he had time off work with a cold. And he had the ideal death – he expired at a party.

PLOT SLOT

Boris Godunov is one of opera's epics, less concerned with focal individuals than with the effects of their ambitions on the course of history. It's all about Tsar Boris's coronation (in 1598), his guilty conscience (he'd ordered the killing of the late Tsar's son, nasty man), his children Xenia and Fyodor, and his own death. Dmitry, that late Tsar's son, survives, however, and his relationship with the Polish princess Marina is an important sub-plot (and gains the support of the Polish people). In fact, The People are a vital constituent, able to react with summary justice on their own behalf.

ABOVE An illustration from Pushkin's tragedy *Boris Godunov*.

LEFT Roerich's set design for the Polovtsian dances, part of *Prince Igor*.

Curious Fact

Rimsky-Korsakov, Mussorgsky, Borodin, and César Cui (1835–1918) each contributed an act to the unperformed opera-ballet *Mlada* in 1872.

A COMPULSIVE MEDDLER

The same goes for *Khovanshchina*, a work about the cruel excesses of Peter the Great. Miraculously so, considering the chaotic state the composer left it in when he died in 1881. *Khovanshchina* was finished and orchestrated by Rimsky-Korsakov, and also later by *Maurice RAVEL* (1875–1937) and *Igor STRAVINSKY* (1882–1971), and yet again by *Dmitry SHOSTAKOVICH* (1906–75). Rimsky-Korsakov was an obsessive cleaner-up of other composers' messes. With *Alexander GLAZUNOV* (1865–1936) he also finished Borodin's powerful epic *Prince Igor*, and tried to improve *Boris Godunov* with his own orchestration, though nowadays opera companies tend to trust Mussorgsky.

1841 The Russian poet Mikhail Lermontov dies in a duel, having championed in his work the "anti-hero."

1851 The first double-decker bus appears on the streets of London.

1868 Russian writer Maxim Gorky is born under the name Aleksei Peshkov at Nizhni Novgorod. He will draw on his own experiences as peddler, servant, gardener, bum, and dock-hand in his writing.

1840~1900

All at Sea

Rimsky-Korsakov

ABOVE Nikolay Andreyevich Rimsky-Korsakov, the arch-tinkerer.

Our arch-meddler-cum-rescuer, the composer of one of the most famous orchestral pieces ever, Scheherazade, *also wrote his own operas. Fifteen of them. They are his most important pieces. RIMSKY-KORSAKOV (1844–1908) was as strong and determined a nationalistic Russian composer as any, following directly in the path of Glinka. But be warned – he's been criticized for his inability to establish characters, though recognized exceptions include Ivan the Terrible in* The Maid of Pskov *and the drunkard Grishka Kuterma in* The Legend of the Invisible City of Kitezh. *For Rimsky, the music always came first, the characterization second. This has made many people look upon his operas as fairy tales played out by puppets – it's a convenient aesthetic viewpoint to take, and certainly pieces with titles like* May Night *(1880) and* Christmas Eve *(1895) sound as though they should be fairy fantasies. And so they are. Rimsky is good at making "fantastic" passages sound fantastic through his use of exotic harmonies. In the process, he maintains Russian opera's reputation for orientalism. Neat.*

LEFT Costume design for *The Tale of Tsar Saltan.*

But Rimsky wasn't always the most fluent of composers. There was a period in mid-career, between about 1882 and 1894, when nothing came from his pen opera-wise. True, this was a time when he was devoting much of his energy to rewritings and to the completion of others' work. But then in 1893 Pyotr Tchaikovsky died, and suddenly Rimsky-Korsakov's operatic energies were renewed – no mere coincidence.

1871 The Royal Albert Hall, built in memory of Prince Albert and seating 10,000, opens. It will house events ranging from the Miss World competition to the Promenade Concerts. Special installations will be added in the roof to combat the bad echo.

1888 The first coast-to-coast crossing of Greenland takes place.

1896 In the Yukon, Canada, the Klondike gold rush gets underway.

ABOVE Program for *Le Coq d'or's* first performance in Moscow, 1909.

TOP OF THE POPS

Rimsky's most popular opera in Russia is *The Tsar's Bride* (1899), though strangely it's one of his least admired everywhere else. Otherwise, the top of the Rimsky pops is *The Golden Cockerel*, finished in 1907 and famously produced by Serge Diaghilev under its French title *Le Coq d'or* in Paris in 1914. Other works worth digging out include *The Maid of Pskov* (1873, but revised twice), *The Snow Maiden* (1882), *Sadko* (1898), *The Tale of Tsar Saltan* (1900), and *The Legend of the Invisible City of Kitezh* (1907). There's also the neat two-acter *Mozart and Salieri* (1898), named after Pushkin's fantasy-tale of the two composers' allegedly murderous conflict. Don't take the story, which has Salieri poisoning Mozart to preserve the even course of art, as gospel.

BELOW Natalia Goncharova's gorgeous set design for Act 1 of *Le Coq d'or*. It had been banned by the government.

In the Navy

Following in the tradition of his father, the first part of R.'s career was spent in the Russian navy. He wrote at least some of his First Symphony between watches, as it were, on a cruise that took him to England, the Baltic, New York, Rio, and the Mediterranean in 1862–5. When he got back from his tour of duty, he became, as he put it, an "officer dilettante" and, under the direction of Mily Balakirev (see p.89), finished the symphony. Composition then took over Rimsky's life, and eventually he was offered the post of professor of composition at St. Petersburg Conservatory.

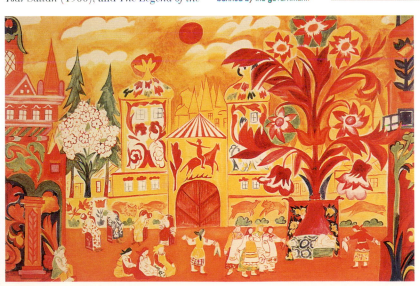

1843 In Paris 'Le Bal des Anglais' is the world's first nightclub to open.

1844 Joseph Smith, founder of the Mormons, and his brother Hyrum are shot dead in Carthage jail, Illinois by 150 masked men who break in.

1853 Henry Steinway and his three sons found the New York firm of piano manufacturers that will become famous worldwide for its concert-grands.

1840~1890
P.I. Tchaikovsky
A Real Pro

With their guru figure Mily BALAKIREV (1837–1910), who didn't write any operas, Mussorgsky, Borodin, Cui, and Rimsky-Korsakov were all members of the informal Russian alliance known as "The Five" or "The Mighty Handful." It's not difficult to spot the absentee: Pyotr Il'yich TCHAIKOVSKY (1840–93) was the most celebrated Russian composer of his generation. Unlike those others, he put himself properly through the musical education system, being among the first graduates of Anton Rubinstein's composition class at the St. Petersburg Conservatory, and never had to earn his living doing anything but composing. A complete pro.

ABOVE Pyotr Il'yich Tchaikovsky, the composer's composer. This portrait was painted shortly before his death in 1893.

In one sense, his ten surviving operas are conservative, because he preserves the old format of set pieces, rather than dabbling with all that new-fangled Wagnerian continuity. But his sure technique, and an awareness of how to attract the public ear, usually – though not always – served him well. As in life, Tchaikovsky's career was a matter of ups and downs.

❝ ☆ ❞

What a Heap!

Dargomïzhsky and Glinka could well have made "The Five" into seven, and the Russian critic Vladimir Stassov decided to employ a more catch-all term of *moguchaya kuchka* – usually translated as "The Mighty Handful" but actually meaning "The Mighty Little Heap."

Who Balakirev?

So who was this Mily Balakirev, who so powerfully influenced these impressionable young composers? A man of some charisma, obviously. His friend Alexander Ulbyshev, a Mozart expert, owned an orchestra, so Balakirev was able to make experiments in orchestration with them. He aspired to a similar nationalism to Glinka, though in Balakirev's case this metamorphosed into a penchant for orientalism. In St. Petersburg, he started the Free School of Music devoted to the nationalist cause; collected and edited native folk tunes; and although he didn't write any operas, he composed incidental music for Shakespeare's *King Lear*.

ABOVE The folk tradition on stage.

1873 Russian bass Fyodor Chaliapin is born to a humble peasant family in Kazan. He will be considered unrivaled as a singing actor, although his realistic acting and robust vocalization will not always be to American tastes.

1881 In the British Army and Navy, flogging is finally abolished.

1885 Russian ballerina Anna Pavlova is born in St. Petersburg. She will become prima ballerina of the Imperial Ballet.

Nadehzda von Meck

Tchaikovsky had a weird relationship with Nadezhda von Meck (he was gay and found her "repulsive"). In 1876, von Meck had written him an admiring letter out of the blue. This precipitated an extraordinary correspondence, in which Tchaikovsky poured out his heart. In return, von Meck sent him a regular allowance, though they never actually met. She was a sort of distant confessor, I suppose, who paid the bill – sounds ideal to me. When the relationship suddenly ceased in 1890, Tchaikovsky became very depressed from then until his controversial death.

RIGHT Scene from the Kirov version of *The Queen of Spades*, Tchaikovsky's take on the Pushkin story.

SUCCESSES AND FAILURES

His most famous opera is *Yevgeny Onegin* (1879). It's a tragic piece (what's new?) about the Byronic Onegin, who, for the sake of his own sense of freedom, turns his back on Tatyana's love and then shoots his best friend Lensky in a duel, caused by his flirting with Lensky's lady, Olga. Its most famous passage – one of the classic opera highlights – is Tatyana's letter scene, but the whole opera is a beautiful, elegant, as well as passionate piece.

Since Tchaikovsky destroyed his first two operas (probably with good reason) – *Voyevoda* (composed in 1868) and *Undina* (composed in 1869) – his first surviving complete opera is the Meyerbeer-influenced *Oprichnik* (1874), and the second *The Snow Maiden* (1873). *The Maid of Orleans* (completed in 1879, revised in 1882) was the first Tchaikovsky opera to travel abroad. Though not a bad effort, it didn't exactly hit the headlines. *Mazeppa* (1884) fared better, enjoying simultaneous productions in Moscow and St. Petersburg, but *The Sorceress* (1887) was, let's face it, a thoroughly deserved failure. However, *The Queen of Spades* (1890), set in the time of Catherine the Great, triumphed. Recordings are available, so why not decide on the merits of these works for yourself.

BELOW Tatyana's fateful letter scene from *Yevgeny Onegin*.

1829 In British-ruled India, *suttee,* the custom whereby an Indian widow burns herself on her husband's funeral pyre, is officially abolished.

1838 Jenny Lind, the "Swedish Nightingale," makes her debut in Stockholm. After a later performance in Vienna she takes 30 curtain calls and the Empress is moved to throw her own bouquet onto the stage in appreciation.

1842 The Bohemian polka becomes a fashionable dance throughout Europe. Smetana makes use of it in his *Bartered Bride.*

1820~1890

Bohemian Rhapsodies
Opera in Middle Europe

ABOVE Bedrich Smetana, considered to be the founder of Czech music.

Glinka wasn't the only composer to worry about establishing native opera in his homeland. In Hungary, for instance, a man called Jószef RUZITSKA (c. 1775–after 1823) wrote a work called Béla's Flight *that was staged in 1822, and Ferenc ERKEL (1810–93) established a Hungarian idiom with a vengeance in a number of works written toward the middle of the 1800s. His* Bánk bán *(1861) still holds Hungarian stages, though it's never seen anywhere else. Composers like András BARTAY (1799–1854), who wrote the first Hungarian comic opera* The Trick *in 1839,*

Milhály MOSONYI (1815–70), and Jenó HUBAY (1858–1937) developed the tradition until the time of BARTÓK (1881–1945). Elsewhere, there was locally inflected opera, but it was Bohemia – after its release from Austrian domination in 1859 – that proved the most important developing ground.

Y ou want names? That of *Frantisek Jan SKROUP* (1801–62) doesn't crop up in many household conversations (he composed a national anthem), but he wrote the first opera, *The Tinker,* to a Czech text in 1826. An opera theater, the Provisional, was built in Prague in 1862; *Bedrich SMETANA* (1824–84) was appointed director in 1866 and wrote half

1858 Frenchman Ferdinand Carré invents the first workable refrigerator, but it will be another 75 years before fridges take over from ice-houses and ice-packs in everyday domestic life.

1873 The Hungarian cities of Buda and Pest are united to form the country's capital.

1883 In New York, the Metropolitan Opera House opens, after various rich businessmen, finding themselves unable to get boxes at the Academy of Music, decide to finance another opera theater in the city and subscribe $800,000.

Bánk-Bán

Ferenc Erkel's historical drama is based on József Katona's play of 1815, set in the thirteenth century, but is really about Hungary's age-old struggle against invading forces. Bánk-Bán is the heroic Palatine of Hungary who kills Gertrud, power-loving wife of King Enre II, for the sake of his country. His wife Melinda, driven insane by the unwelcome attentions of Gertrud's brother Otto, also dies; Bánk asks to be buried with her.

a dozen works during his eight-year tenure, including his most famous, *The Bartered Bride* (1866). It was a vivid, brilliant folk opera, and was followed by others: *The Kiss* (1876), *The Secret* (1878), and more seriously, *Libuse* (1881), following the epic revolutionary *Dalibor* (1868).

BELOW Folk-inspired costume design for the 1928 version of Smetana's *The Bartered Bride*.

THE TREND SPREADS

Antonín DVORÁK (1841–1904), he of the "New World" Symphony, followed Smetana's example with *The Cunning Peasant* (1878), *The Devil and Kate* (1899), and the fairytale *Rusalka* (1901). Others, like *Zdenek* FIBICH (1850–1900), continued the development, as did the young Leos Janácek – but more of him later. Poland, Bulgaria, and the Baltic countries all cultivated their own national operatic styles, as did the Scandinavian countries, heavily influenced by Wagner. Toward the end of the century there were also stirrings in the United States, and the British operatic renaissance had begun in the conspicuously Teutonic *The Wreckers* by the redoubtable *Ethel* SMYTH (1858–1944). Nowhere was now safe.

Carl Nielsen (1865–1931)

The Danish composer Carl Nielsen – humble beginnings, honest but always original music – wrote two operas, *Saul and David* (1902) and *Maskarade* (1906): as different as could be in style and matter. One is a tragic biblical confrontation, the other a social comedy. But they share a fascination with (old cliché, I know) the human condition. *Maskarade*, after Ludvig Holberg's 1724 play, is full of simple tunes and naïve rhymes, but it's not a simplistic opera. Indeed, it touches on issues of freedom, equality, and death: no laughing matter, but such food for thought is the best kind of comedy there is. *Saul and David* is deeply serious and highly charged dramatic realization, influenced by Wagner and by late Verdi. Difficult to catch a live performance outside Denmark (Danish not being a common singing language to any but the Danes). There are recordings of both pieces, however.

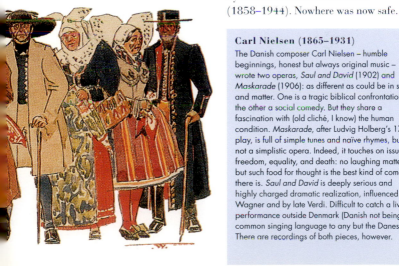

1869 The postcard is invented by Emmanual Hermann of Vienna, who proposes a "postal telegram" sent at a lower cost than a normal letter with envelope.

1884 Sigmund Freud is one of the first Europeans to study cocaine, suggesting that it might be a pain-relieving agent.

1900 Ferdinand von Zeppelin's first cigar-shaped vessel, known as a dirigible balloon but soon to take his name, rises into the air.

1860~1950
Rich, Radical, *and* Conservative
Richard Strauss

ABOVE Strauss, composer of *Heldenleben*, in decadent mode.

Question: what happened in Germany as a result of the all-pervasive Wagner? Answer: Richard STRAUSS *(1864–1949). He came to opera quite late, in the 1890s, but it was always inevitable that he would become a musician of some sort, since his father was a horn player in the Munich Court Orchestra. There was money in the family, too, and these privileges facilitated the publication and performance of works written when Strauss was still a teenager. Then Hans von Bülow – conductor, critic, and former husband of Wagner's wife – invited Strauss at 21 to become assistant conductor of the Meiningen Court Orchestra. Until the mid-1920s, he earned his living mainly from conducting.*

His early music was unaffected by Wagner, since his father disapproved, but inevitably once he was independent Strauss cultivated many contacts, and wrote a number of symphonic poems as well as *Guntram* (1894) for Weimar. The one-act *Feuersnot* (1901) followed this early effort, and then – bang! – two murderous shockers, *Salome* (text: Oscar Wilde) and *Elektra* (text: Hugo von Hofmannsthal), in 1905 and 1909. These were above all psychological studies, their language dense, complex, and significantly chromatic, rather than tonal. Strauss's music seemed to totter on the edge of an anarchic abyss.

ABOVE Richard Strauss at the conductor's podium; he wielded the baton before he took up his pen to write.

1908 Serge Diaghilev presents *Boris Godunov* in Paris; three years later his Ballet Russe will be formed and will incorporate contributions from many of the foremost composers, artists, and dancers of the time.

1912 Germany claims to possess 30,000 millionaires.

1950 No shortage of roses to choose from for your garden: 30,000 different varieties are cataloged, but silver ones…?

ABOVE Title page for *Salome*, the naughty piece of decadence written by Oscar Wilde.

PLOT SLOT

Der Rosenkavalier: the young Oktavian is loved by the rather older Feldmarschallin, while Baron Ochs plans to marry Sophie. Oktavian, disguised as a maid, "Mariandel," attracts Ochs' attentions. He takes the traditional Silver Rose to Sophie for Ochs, and falls for her. Ochs gets a letter suggesting an assignation with "Mariandel." Oktavian springs his trap! Ochs is shamed, the Feldmarschallin gives up her toy boy, and the lovers are united.

BACK FROM THE BRINK

What did he do? He stepped back, composing *Der Rosenkavalier* (1911), a comedy of manners, with touches of pastiche and identifiable arias within its continuous music. It's a much-loved work (but not by me). Like the less successful *Ariadne auf Naxos* (1912) and *Die Frau ohne Schatten* (1919), *Der Rosenkavalier*'s text was again by Hofmannsthal, who also provided the words for *Die aegyptische Helena* (1928) and *Arabella* (1933). These operas, rather lofty in manner, were punctuated by the autobiographical *Intermezzo* (1924, with Strauss's own text), in an attempt to be more in tune with the prevailing musical fashion. *Die schweigsame Frau* (1935), *Friedenstag* (1938), *Daphne* (1938), and *Die Liebe der Danae* (written in 1940) followed. During this time Strauss was accused of co-operating with the Nazis, though counterclaims have been made that he helped Jewish friends and relatives and that he was, in fact, apolitical. The jury will always be out on this one.

Strauss couldn't repeat the success of *Rosenkavalier*. Not, anyway, until 1942 with *Capriccio*, whose topic is the age-old battle between music and words. The opera seems to me to be uncomfortably middle class, as well as reactionary. But that's heresy. Strauss is adored.

Which Strauss Is Which?

No problem if it's *Salome* or *Elektra* – Richard Strauss's language is grotesque, violent, weird, lurching. But all the Strausses wrote a lot of waltzy music in 3/4 time. The true test is this: if its tread seems just a little heavy, then it's Richard; if it sparkles, then it's one of the others. Take pot luck between Johann (1804–49, composer of the Radetzky March); his sons Johann II (1825–99, *Die Fledermaus* and the Blue Danube), Josef (1827–70), and Eduard (1835–1916). (Richard wasn't related.) One further clue: the related Strausses didn't write operas, and Richard didn't write operettas or self-contained waltzes, polkas, or marches.

1862 Louis Pasteur makes the most important discovery (up to now) in the history of medicine – that germs cause disease. His theory will eventually result in longer life expectancy and a population explosion.

1885 British scientist Francis Galton discovers that no two people's fingerprints are the same.

1893 "Art Nouveau" appears in Europe, characterized by sinuous lines representing stylized flowers and foliage.

1860~1915

Debussy's Tour de Force
Pelléas and Mélisande

Now this is more to my liking. Pelléas et Mélisande, *Claude Debussy's only finished opera, was first seen in 1902. It's the work of a rebel. The*

ABOVE Romantic setting for doomed lovers.

almighty Wagner had become god of the French operatic establishment, but his way was not Debussy's. Which is not to say that DEBUSSY *(1862–1918) was entirely unaffected by the moods Wagner conjured – on the contrary. Lack of imitation does not mean lack of admiration. For some time Debussy was looking for a language in which "rhythms cannot be contained in bars," "themes suggest orchestral colors," and "there is no theory, you just have to listen, and the law is fantasy." Quite the anarchist, wasn't he?*

Well, no. *Pelléas*, a setting of Maurice Maeterlinck's eponymous play, is a model of concentration and intensity, spare in texture, plain and speechlike in melody, but incredibly cleverly and subtly structured, and intoxicatingly powerful. It expresses to perfection the simple tale of the illicit love affair woven between the strange girl Mélisande and Pelléas in and around the mysterious castle – a Gallic equivalent to Wagner's *Tristan* in fact.

FAR-REACHING INFLUENCE

Debussy worked hard at getting opera right. His work-list includes several abandoned music dramas, including settings of Edgar Allen Poe's *The Fall of the House of Usher* and *The Devil in the Belfry*. But with *Pelléas* he hit the nail on

the head. It was to influence opera – and music in general – profoundly. Without *Pelléas*, for instance, two twentieth-century masterpieces, Bartók's *Duke Bluebeard's Castle* and Berg's *Wozzeck*, would not have been the same.

1900 Freud's *The Interpretation of Dreams* gives new meaning to dreams as truths that human beings cannot perhaps accept in their waking hours.

1907 In New York, the first *Ziegfeld Follies*, based on the *Folies Bergères* and designed to "glorify the American girl," burst onto the stage.

1915 The remains of Rouget de Lisle, composer of the "Marseillaise," are brought to the Invalides in Paris.

Other Pelléases

There are three other *Pelléas and Mélisandes*, but none of them is actually an opera. Fauré's is incidental musical for an English production of Maeterlinck's play (seen in London's Prince of Wales Theatre in 1898). Sibelius's is also fine incidental music, composed in 1905 and turned into a self-contained suite that year. Best of all, there's Schoenberg's immense symphonic poem – nothing incidental about this – which was composed in 1903. It's Wagnerian in scope and structure – and in some ways in sound as well. Traditional harmony and keys still have their function.

ABOVE Ravel only wrote two operas, but both are enchanting.

BELOW Thomas Allen as Pelléas and Anne Howell as Mélisande in the Royal Opera's 1978 production.

> " ★ "
>
> ### Debussy Speaks
>
> Here are a couple of other gems uttered by Debussy regarding *Pelléas*. "Music in opera is far too predominant." "No discussion or argument between the characters, whom I see at the mercy of life and fate." Say no more.

Debussy's greatest French contemporary was *Maurice RAVEL* (1875–1937), whose *L'heure espagnole* (1911) is a sparkling comedy, but whose one-act opera *L'enfant et les sortilèges* (1925) qualifies as one of the most exquisite, and poignant, scores of the century.

Maurice Maeterlinck (1862–1949)

The Belgian poetic dramatist Maeterlinck first established himself as a leading Symbolist with his play *La Princesse Maleine* in 1889. But it is *Pelléas et Mélisande* (1894) for which he is now best known, and not only because of Debussy's opera. *L'Oiseau-bleu* was also a great success in 1908; and there are telling philosophical essays. Generally, he drew on traditions of romance and fairy tale, but surrounded them with a dark, brooding atmosphere and with melancholy.

1878 Electric street lighting illuminates London, while at Gotha in Germany light of another kind is shed, as the first European crematorium is established.

1889 At a hunting lodge at Mayerling, the Austrian crown prince and his lover are found shot dead – the official verdict of suicide is countered by rumors that they were murdered.

1901 Ragtime jazz becomes popular in America – it will undergo a revival in the 1970s when Scott Joplin's music is used for the film *The Sting*.

1870~1930

Berg and Schoenberg
The Struggle for Expression

Three composers dominate the large circle that we have come to know as the Second Viennese School, which flourished in the first half of the twentieth century – Arnold SCHOENBERG (1874–1951), Alban BERG (1885–1935), and Anton WEBERN (1883–1945). Webern didn't actually write operas, but many others in this loose alliance did. Alexander VON ZEMLINSKY (1872–1942) and Franz SCHREKER (1878–1934) are two of those whose works are well worth exploring. In Germany you can even see them occasionally, praise be!

BELOW Alban Berg, composer of the libidinous *Lulu*, painted by Arnold Schoenberg.

Schoenberg's One-act Operas

Schoenberg wrote three one-act operas: *Erwartung* (1909) is an expressionist study of the inner mind; *Die glückliche Hand* (1913) is more emotionally removed, less psychologically tangled, and was presented in 1924, with lighting influenced by the theories of Schoenberg's friend Vassily Kandinsky; *Von heute auf Morgen* (1929) is a rather heavy-handed comedy about modern marriage.

Schoenberg, of course, is music's eternal *bête noire*, because he threw out the old system of keys and introduced serial music, in which theoretically every note in the chromatic scale has an equal place in the hierarchy. No key, "tonic" note, no dominant, sub-dominant, or leading note to define structural functions. Why did he do such a thing? Because he wanted to express himself as perfectly as possible. He'd tried everything in order to do that – he started by composing in a post-Wagnerian, tonal language. He went on to write atonally, using just his ears (this his most psychologically searching and powerful music). And then, still not satisfied, he evolved serialism, applying it to reinterpretations of old forms. Eventually, after moving to the United States, Schoenberg returned, from time to time, to tonality.

His opera *Moses und Aron*, composed in 1930–2, is about precisely the problem of expressing oneself. Aron is the verbal channel for Moses' visions. But perfect

1916 Tanks are introduced during the Battle of the Somme but are at first used timidly.

1925 A copy of the Bible costs just $3 now, compared with the equivalent of $2,000 in the fourteenth century.

1941 English aviatrix Amy Johnson dies, after baling out into the estuary of the River Thames.

Lulu: Plays and Films

First, an interesting fact. Yes, there's another *Lulu*, a Romantic opera of 1824 (really a *Singspiel*) by the Danish composer Friedrich Kuhlau (1786–1832). But back to the *Lulu* based on Wedekind's two plays: *Erdgeist* and *Die Büchse von Pandora*. The Austrian filmmaker Georg Wilhelm Pabst made a *film noir* version of the former. Stephen Spender translated both plays into English as *Earth Spirit* and *Pandora's Box*. And recently the jazz composer Jon Faddis made a version seen in Spoleto, U.S.A.

expression is a difficult objective and Schoenberg failed to finish the piece. In performance, the moment when it stops – with Moses uttering, "O word, word that I lack" as he is left alone by Aron and the marching Israelites (who have replaced the Golden Calf with what Moses sees as another idol, the tables of law) – is very poignant. All through the opera there is potent tension between what is felt and what is said. And, crucially, Moses' is a speaking role, whereas Aron sings.

EXPRESSING COMPASSION

Alban Berg studied with Schoenberg, but is a quite different composer, evolving a language that was based on Schoenberg's serialism but freely alluded to tonality and to a ripe, Romantic, even nostalgic expression. He wrote two operas, *Wozzeck* (1925) and *Lulu* (begun in 1929, but left with its final act unfinished at Berg's death in 1935; it was completed by Friedrich Cerha only in the 1970s). *Wozzeck*, after Georg Büchner's drama, is about a soldier's collision with fate, self-delusion, and enduring the system. *Lulu*, after two plays by Frank Wedekind, charts the fall of another victim of circumstance who happens to be a *femme fatale*. Its completion was crucial; it turns out to be an arch-shaped work, with a film scene – and a musical palindrome – at its heart. It is powerful, disturbing, darkly beautiful stuff.

LEFT Dramatic scene from the Théâtre de Chatelet 1995 version of Schoenberg's *Moses und Aron*, with Philip Langridge and Aage Haugland.

The First Viennese School

Mozart, Beethoven, and Schubert were the principal members of what was never actually called the First Viennese School (and wasn't, of course, an actual school), but they were based in Vienna and helped to propel it to the forefront of Europe's musical life. Today, Vienna is a hive of much bold, even experimental, compositional activity. So when you go there, watch out. It's not all *Sachertorte*.

1888 Gustav Mahler becomes musical director of the Budapest Opera, but will resign after two years due to insuperable difficulties.

1902 Enrico Caruso makes a gramophone recording and becomes the first real "gramophone" tenor.

1912 Carl Gustav Jung publishes his work *The Psychology of the Unconscious* and gradually becomes increasingly critical of Freud.

1880~1940

Bartók and Kodály

Bluebeard and *Háry János*

ABOVE Béla Bartók at the piano, playing his "difficult" music to an unenthusiastic American audience in 1938.

A few pages back I wrote that Béla Bartók's Duke Bluebeard's Castle *(1911) wouldn't have been possible without Debussy's* Pelléas et Mélisande. *And so it wouldn't.* Bluebeard, *based on a traditional Magyar tale, is an opera of symbolism and expressionism just as much as* Pelléas *is. It's a sinister search into the soul of Judith, who is drawn into Bluebeard's intoxicatingly mysterious, dark world, unable to resist looking behind the seven closed doors, into his own black soul. The consequences, when he opens the final door, are inevitable.*

The music of this psycho-drama – Jung would have a field day analyzing its meanings – is richer than Debussy's, the atmosphere heavier, more claustrophobic. In fact, it is influenced by the kind of textures familiar from Richard Strauss, though, as always with Bartók – at whatever stage of his composing career – it is also highly individual.

Duke Bluebeard's Castle is one of the essential operas. And, conveniently for the harassed executive eager to improve his or her operatic knowledge, it's also short – only one act – so the sustained concentration required is not too demanding. Curiously, Bartók wrote no further operas. In 1940 he emigrated to the U.S., where his health began to fail and he died five years later of leukemia.

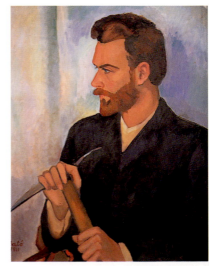

ABOVE Zoltán Kodály as a dashing young man; he was in full folk-song-collecting mode at this period in his life.

1917 Austrian Wagner von Jauregg resorts to the unlikely solution of treating syphilitic paralysis by injecting patients with malaria.

1925 The cloche hat comes into its own in hiding a multitude of wayward hairstyles.

1938 Two Hungarian brothers, Ladislao and Georg Biro, invent that useful instrument, the ball-point pen.

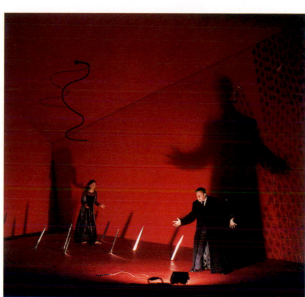

ABOVE Scary, blood-spattered 1993 version of Bartók's *Bluebeard's Castle* with Sally Burgess as Judith and Gwynne Howell as the wicked Duke.

Who is Háry János?

He's an old soldier. And in Kodály's opera – strictly, let it be noted, a *Singspiel* – he shows off about his youthful deeds in the local inn. They're a bit exaggerated.... Apparently, he rescued Maria Luisa, daughter of Kaiser Franz, on the Russian–Austrian border, went to Vienna, was nominated a General, won a battle single-handed against Napoleon, won the love of the Emperor's wife, but chose to remain true to his village bride and to his village.

Bluebeard

The Bluebeard story has long fascinated writers with its tale – based on the life of the French Marshal Gilles de Rais (1404–40) – of the Duke who murdered six wives for disobeying his command not to enter a locked room, before himself being killed before he could bump off Wife No. 7. The story was popularized by French writer Charles Perrault in 1697 in his inimitable fairy tale *Contes de ma mère l'oye*, and has proved a rich source for those with fertile imaginations ever since.

HUNGARIAN COMEDY

Hungarian opera's standard was also carried by Bartók's great friend *Zoltán Kodály* (1882–1967), whose *Háry János* (1926) is a comedy quite at odds with the flavor of Bartók's work. Alas, it's rarely staged – all those Puccinis getting in the way again – and most music lovers are familiar with the piece only through the popular orchestral suite that Kodály drew from it. That's something, I suppose. Kodály also collaborated with Bartók on a folk-song collection, the first volume appearing in 1951.

1854 The Immaculate Conception of the Blessed Virgin Mary is declared by Pope Pius IX to be an article of faith.

1863 In America, roller skating is introduced.

1895 Thomas Masaryk, who will be first president of the Czech Republic, writes *The Czech Question*.

1850~1925

Small Ideas, Great Music

Janácek

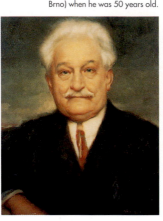

BELOW Leos Janácek; he came late to opera, *Jenufa* being first performed (in his home town of Brno) when he was 50 years old.

Leos Janácek's first two operas, Sárka *(composed in 1888) and* The Beginning of Romance *(1894) continued, as you might expect, very much in the nationalistic ways of Dvorák and Smetana. But with* Jenufa *(finished in 1903 and performed with considerable success in January 1904), JANÁCEK (1854–1928) made giant strides, dispensing with ensembles, duets and set numbers in favor of continuous monologue, conversation, and symbolic chorus in this tale, set in a Moravian village, of steamy passion and jealousy.*

Janácek was born in Moravia, the son of a schoolmaster and organist, but despite studying in Leipzig and Vienna he remained in Brno for about 30 years, where he started composing mostly choral pieces. The influence of local folksong injected a new individuality into his music, and he evolved a "speech-melody" theory, writing down in musical notation the natural inflections of words and phrases he heard in different situations. Increasingly, the orchestral and the voice parts in his operas became, as it were, semi-detached, with the orchestra underpinning and unifying the drama through Janácek's characteristic obsessive exploitation of small ideas.

SMALL BUT PERFECTLY FORMED

Jenufa took some time to establish itself, but when it received its Prague premiere in 1916 it effectively put its composer on the musical map. A sequence of brilliant operas followed in the last decade of his

Janácek's Secret

After the belated premiere of *Jenufa*, Leos Janácek had a secret love, in the person of Kamila Stosslová, the wife of an antique dealer, who was 38 years younger than he. He wrote to her almost every day (a total of over 600 letters) and in his last year kept a diary devoted to her. But there was no reciprocation, and not much threat to Janácek's marriage. One might think of the one-sided infatuation as an old man's folly. Good luck to him!

1903 Space suits, satellites, and the possibility of a space station get their first airing by Russian physicist Konstantin Eduardovich Tsiolkovsky.

1908 Isadora Duncan's style of dancing becomes increasingly popular; but she herself will suffer the suicide of her husband, the death of her children, and her own accidental strangling.

1923 Child prodigy Yehudi Menuhin appears as a soloist with the San Francisco Symphony Orchestra at the age of just seven.

life. *The Excursions of Mr. Broucek* (1920) bizarrely portrays a man transported to the moon and then to the fifteenth century; *Kátya Kabanová* (1921) is a moving tragedy culminating in the heroine's suicide; *The Cunning Little Vixen* (1924) is an animal tale without the cutesy Bambi syndrome; *The Makropoulos Case* (1926) investigates the feelings of a woman who has prolonged her life by 300 years; *From the House of the Dead* (unfinished) is a chilling sequence of events from Dostoyevsky's prison-camp novel. All these works are to the point, short but intense, powerful and perfectly formed.

PLOT SLOT

Steva, the mill-owner, and his half-brother Laca both love Jenufa, their orphaned cousin brought up by the Kostelnicka, or sacristan (a lady). Jenufa loves Steva and indeed is pregnant by him. The Kostelnicka says that they can't marry until Steva's been sober for a year. In a jealous rage, Laca slashes Jenufa's cheek and she is disfigured for life. When she gives birth to Steva's child, the Kostelnicka lies that the child has died, then has to make the lie true. Jenufa accepts Laca's proposal of marriage, while Steva arrives at the pre-nuptials with his own betrothed and Jenufa brokers a reconciliation. All seem happy. Then tumult. Workers have discovered the corpse of the child, frozen in the river where the Kostelnicka placed him. Jenufa forgives her. She thinks Laca will no longer want her, but she is wrong...and we all go home in tears.

NAMES TO NOTE

Bohuslav Martinu *(1890–1959) is the most famous other Czech, but he settled in Paris in 1923 and wrote for international audiences. Other post-Dvořák Czech composers include* **Jaromír Weinberger,** *famous for* Schvanda the Bagpiper *(1927),* **Josef Foerster** *(1859–1951),* **Vitezslav Novák** *(1870–1949),* **Otakar Jeremiás** *(1892–1962),* **Alois Hába** *(1893–1973),* **Karel Kovarovic** *(1862–1920),* **Otakar Ostrcil** *(1879–1935),* **Frantisek Neumann** *(1874–1929),* **Zdenek Fibich** *(1850–1900)...mostly just names in books like this one, but worth investigating if you come across their work.*

RIGHT Lesley Garrett in foxy mode as the eponymous Cunning Little Vixen in the English National Opera's 1996 revival.

1906 Women internationally are forbidden to undertake night-shift work.

1916 Rasputin is lured to the Yusupov Palace in St. Petersburg by a group of noblemen, poisoned and – when that fails – shot and his body thrown into the canal.

1934 With the ideal of performing opera in a beautiful setting, and inspired by his wife, soprano Audrey Mildmay, John Christie builds an opera house in the grounds of his home at Glyndebourne, Sussex and England's annual Glyndebourne festival is born.

1900~1940

Shostakovich and Social Realism
The Scandalous *Lady Macbeth*

ABOVE Early photograph of Dmitry Shostakovich, whose realism was too real for Stalin.

Under Lenin, composers in the new Soviet Union enjoyed their freedom, and none more so than the young Dmitry SHOSTAKOVICH (1906–75). He was an adventurous composer, a member of the Association for Contemporary Music, which actively encouraged the study and performance of contemporary Western composers. So when the satirical opera The Nose *was premiered in 1930, applying – and considerably advancing – the "musical realist" principles of Alexander DARGOMÏZHSKY (1813–69), there was no reason for him to fear the censor's admonitions. But then Lenin died, and Stalin came to power. In 1932 all musical activity was brought under state control. Experimentation was out; populism was definitely in.*

Shostakovich had already nearly finished his second opera, *The Lady Macbeth of the Mtsensk District*, the first of an intended trilogy about Russian women. After its premiere in 1934, the opera was hailed as a shining example of Socialist Realism, and there were 83 performances in Leningrad and 97 in Moscow. But in 1936 Stalin went to see it and shortly afterward *Pravda* carried a stinging editorial denouncing the piece as "Chaos instead of music." *Lady Macbeth* disappeared from the repertoire until 1963, when it

LEFT A rapacious Stalin seizes France (for her own good, of course) in this contemporary cartoon.

1940 Walt Disney releases the film of *Pinocchio*, the tale of the elongating nose.

1941 Shostakovich acts as a firefighter during the siege of Leningrad.

1960 A supersonic American U-2 plane is shot down by the Soviets, who accuse the Americans (correctly) of spying.

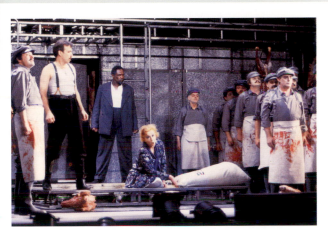

LEFT Lady Macbeth of the Mtsensk District gets her hands dirty in a 1987 performance by the English National Opera with Josephine Barstow (Katerina) and Willard White (Boris).

reappeared, heavily modified, as *Katerina Ismaylova* (the original version took another whole decade to resurface). Shostakovich also withdrew his Fourth Symphony, for fear of causing further offense to the frankly artistically illiterate dictator.

Dargomïzhsky

I know we're well into the twentieth century, but we mustn't forget the influence of Alexander Dargomïzhsky. Okay, he wasn't the towering figure that Glinka was, but he had more or less the same aims. He was apparently a man of biting humor, who in 1843 resigned his government job, went to Brussels and Paris, and became fascinated by the "lower" musical-theatrical forms and by the petty criminal fraternity that he saw passing through the courts. And he started experimenting with Russian speech rhythms and intonations, leading to *The Stone Guest*, the only opera of his four to retain a reputation – and that more for its influence in the twentieth century than for its intrinsic qualities – into our times. Most of his contemporaries and immediate successors preferred his version of *Rusalka* (1856), to be honest. Fat chance we'll ever get of seeing that.

Lady Macbeth is a powerful and important work, fast-paced, richly allusive to other theatrical traditions like the circus, yet realistic and digestible in its portrayal of the tragedy of the misguided Katerina, who poisons her father-in-law, strangles her husband, kills a rival and, ultimately, herself. But it proved to be the premature last throw in Shostakovich's operatic career. Sad, or what?

Socialist Realism

The artistic doctrine espoused by Stalin dictated that Soviet society should be portrayed in glowing, optimistic, patriotic, Socialist terms. It was applied right across the arts, from music to the visual arts and writing, and was exemplified by novels such as *How the Steel was Tempered* (1932–4) by Nikolay Ostrovsky. Those who fell foul of its rigid constraints or failed to toe the strict Stalinist party line were censored as being too "modern" and included Shostakovich, and the writers Alexander Solzhenitsyn and Mikhail Sholokhov.

1890 Vyacheslav Molotov, who will become known for an explosive "cocktail," is born in Russia.

1914 St. Petersburg's identity crisis starts: it becomes Petrograd; then Leningrad; then back to St. Petersburg…

1927 Russian Lev Theremin introduces the first electronic "space-controlled" musical instrument to the U.S. – not controlled by little green men but by movements of the hands, which do not touch the instrument.

1890~1950

The Rebel Who Returned
Prokofiev's Oranges and Angels

ABOVE Eclectic food for Prokofiev's operatic thought.

Even more so than the headstrong young Shostakovich, Sergei PROKOFIEV (1891–1953) was in his early years a radical, and reacted strongly to some of the teachings of his mentor, Rimsky-Korsakov. Two early operas – Maddalena *(1913) and* The Gambler *(1917, later revised) – were written in Russia, but after the Russian Revolution, Prokofiev went to live in America, then Paris. On the Atlantic voyage he passed the time by reading Carlo Gozzi's play* Amore delle tre Melarance – *a wild, absurd, supernatural comedy. His imagination was fired by it. The result?* The Love for Three Oranges, *staged for the first time in Chicago in 1921. It's a brilliant, vibrant piece, a potent mix of Rimsky and the early Stravinsky ballets.*

But even before it had been seen, Prokofiev was working on a completely different piece, *The Fiery Angel*, which was a little more serious. Its subject? Devil possession and religious mania in sixteenth-century Germany – the sort of story of which controversial British film director Ken Russell might approve. The music is garish and spiky, the plot fixed upon the possessed Renata. It's a striking piece, but, most observers agree, hardly the most perfectly balanced opera of all time.

Although it was finished in 1927, *The Fiery Angel* wasn't performed until 1954. In the meantime, in the early 1930s Prokofiev made several visits to Stalin's Soviet Union and eventually – incredibly –

1936 Prokofiev's "Peter and the Wolf" is first performed at Moscow Children's Theater Center.

1941 There is a shortage of oranges (among other things) in wartime Britain.

1951 The U.S. produces about 400,000 pounds of penicillin during the course of the year.

Prokofiev's Life and Times

Sergei Prokofiev was a rebellious young man and allied himself with the avant-garde movement, causing uproar with his explosive early works. But in exile, in America and in Paris, his language became softer, the harmonies more graceful. Back in Stalin's Soviet Union, for a time the lyrical aspects of his music blossomed, though the demands of the state also led to some stirringly patriotic, but pretty vacuous, scores.

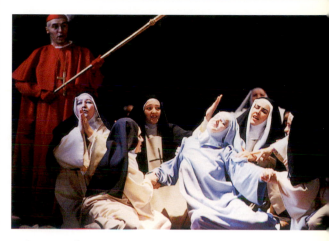

BELOW A chorus of approval from the 1989 staging of *The Love for Three Oranges*, Prokofiev's glorious homage to citrus fruit.

ABOVE Renata surrenders to her possessions in the luridly sensational, but seldom performed, *Fiery Angel*.

decided to return permanently in 1936, whereupon his music took on significantly more conservative leanings… There was a comic opera, *The Duenna*, in 1941, but from this time on Prokofiev suffered the same problems as Shostakovich, incurring official displeasure at the lack of triumphalism in his Sixth Symphony, for instance. Had he stayed in the West, who knows what else might have come from his fertile mind? As it was, he died on the same day as Stalin, his spirits broken.

PLOT SLOT

The prince in *The Love for Three Oranges* can be cured of his melancholy only by laughter. Fata Morgana fails at every attempt until she falls over and he finally succumbs. Finding three oranges in a kitchen, the prince takes them into the desert, where each opens to show a princess. While two die of thirst, the third is revived with a bucket of water and united with the prince.

1911 Eurythmics (the system of rhythmic gymnastics, not the pop group) becomes more widespread as Emile Jaques-Dalcroze founds his institute for teaching it in Germany.

1917 The largest telescope in the world, with a diameter of 100 inches, is installed at Mount Wilson in California – it will remain the largest for three decades.

1929 Hindemith's *Neues vom Tage* shocks Hitler for its scene of the soprano in the bath.

1910~1950

Opera and Nazi Germany

Hindemith, Weill, and Other "Degenerates"

ABOVE Berthold Brecht (1898–1956), anti-Nazi dramatist and sometime librettist to Kurt Weill.

While Strauss was plowing his conservative furrows and the New Viennese composers were doing their thing, Paul HINDEMITH (1895–1963), Kurt WEILL (1900–50), and a whole host of Germanic composers (I include Austrian here) were working at their own operatic forms. Hindemith, a violinist, led the Frankfurt Opera Orchestra for several years from 1915. As a composer he fell in with the neo-classical stream of thought propagated in the 1920s by Stravinsky and others. His first full-length opera, Cardillac *(1926) – not to be confused with an American car or anything to do with heart problems – is decidedly not of Romantic bent.*

His most famous opera is *Mathis der Maler* (completed in 1935), loosely based on the life of the painter Matthias Grünewald (*c.*1475–1528), but actually about what it's like to be an artist in society and how to have the courage to be true to yourself. Big subject. And a huge, brave, and effective piece, with deep characterization. Shortly after the opera was written, Hindemith's music was condemned by the Nazis. In 1938 he left Germany and two years later settled in the United States, but returned to Europe in 1953 to work on a projected opera about the astronomer Johann Kepler, entitled *Die Harmonie der Welt* (1957). Other operas include *Der lange Weihnachtsmahl* (1961), Hindemith's own tribute to America.

LEFT *Volksoper: The Threepenny Opera*, Brecht/Weill's take on John Gay's satirical, demotic *Beggar's Opera*. It really annoyed Hitler.

1933 Around 60,000 artists – musicians among them – emigrate from Germany between now and 1939.

1945 A B-25 bomber hits floors 78–9 of the Empire State Building in New York.

1954 The first successful kidney transplant is performed using identical twins; the recipient lives for another eight years.

A POLITICAL MESSAGE

Kurt Weill's early language owed something to Schoenberg and *Ferruccio* Busoni (1866–1924), as his one-act opera *Der Protagonist* (1926) demonstrates. But when he began a collaboration with the dramatist Berthold Brecht in 1927, everything changed. Now he used tonality and a popular cabaret style, with biting irony to point out the evils of capitalism. Brecht's lyrics and the singing of Austrian-born Lotte Lenya (1905–81), who married Weill (twice), now played a major role in his work. Operatic pieces couched in this manner include *Die Dreigroschenoper (The Threepenny Opera,* 1928),

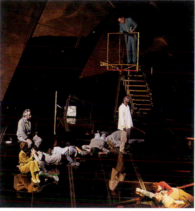

ABOVE *Mathis der Maler,* the Hindemith opera banned by the Nazis in 1934, here seen in 1995.

Aufstiegund Fall der Stadt Mahoganny (1930), and *Die sieben Todsünden* (1933). Those popular songs like "Mack the Knife," from *The Threepenny Opera,* may be celebrated in their own right, but ought really to be heard – and seen – in context. Not surprisingly, Weill was declared *persona non grata* and, like Hindemith, left Berlin in 1933. Once settled in the United States, he immersed himself in composing for Broadway musicals, which is where we must leave him.

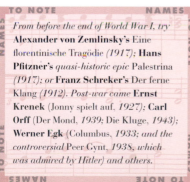

TO NOTE   NAMES

From before the end of World War I, try **Alexander von Zemlinsky's** Eine florentinische Tragödie *(1917);* **Hans Pfitzner's** *quasi-historic epic* Palestrina *(1917); or* **Franz Schreker's** Der ferne Klang *(1912). Post-war came* **Ernst Krenek** (Jonny spielt auf, *1927);* **Carl Orff** (Der Mond, *1939;* Die Kluge, *1943);* **Werner Egk** (Columbus, *1933; and the controversial* Peer Gynt, *1938, which was admired by Hitler) and others.*

Entartete Musik

Other German and Austrian composers (as well as those of other European countries invaded by Hitler) did not manage to leave Nazi Germany in time. Those of Jewish descent or sympathies were of course particularly badly treated. Many were derided as composers of *entartete Musik* – "degenerate music" – and held up as such in a Düsseldorf exhibition so named in 1938. (Bartók, outraged, courageously demanded that his name be included on the list.) Many died in the horror of the concentration camps. Ernst Krenek (b.1900), Erich Korngold (1897–1957), and Berthold Goldschmidt (b.1903) all survived to enjoy late careers, but Viktor Ullmann (1898–c.1944), Pavel Haas, Hans Krása, Gideon Klein... the roll call of those who perished is harrowing.

1882 70 years after Napoleon's retreat from Moscow, Tchaikovsky's *1812 Overture* thunders out in celebration.

1909 Hair perms, given for the first time by London hairdressers, revolutionize the appearance of a nation.

1914 On 1 September the last of the passenger pigeons to fly across American skies in their tens of millions, dies in Cincinnati Zoo.

1880~1960

Stravinsky at the Opera House
The Rake's Progress

Russian-born, temporarily Parisian and finally American, Igor STRAVINSKY *(1882–1971) was one of those composers who could live just about anywhere and write just about anything, putting his personal stamp on any style. His ballet* The Rite of Spring *caused a riot at its premiere in 1913 and there were several other dramatic pieces in his canon – and not only ballets. The burlesque* Renard *(1916), for example, and* The Soldier's Tale *(to be read, played, and danced) of 1918. Or, at around the same time,* Les noces *– "choreographic scenes" with solo vocalists and choir. And so on, up to and including the ballets* Orpheus *(1947) and* Agon *(1957) and Stravinsky's final musical play for television,* The Flood *(1962) – altogether different from the snazzy style of* The Rite, Petrushka *(1911), and* The Firebird *(1910).*

**Hogarth's
*Rake's Progress***
We tend to think of William Hogarth in terms of lines and hatches, but in fact his original series of engravings were made from his original paintings, executed in 1735. He stated once that his aim was to paint and engrave moral subjects, to "compose pictures on canvas similar to representations on the stage" and to treat his subjects as a dramatic writer would. Such a stance makes his work as ripe for operatic treatment as any novel or play. And Hogarth also performed a signal service for fellow-artists by campaigning for a Copyright Act to be passed (1735).

LEFT Phase eight in the progress of the original Rake, by Hogarth (1733); Tom Rakewell languishes in Bedlam.

1930 Friedrich Trautwein of Berlin invents the Tratonium, an electronic instrument that enables the player to obtain a variety of tone-color.

1942 The "National Loaf" is introduced to wartime Britain.

1961 In the spaceship *Vostok I*, Yuri Gagarin circles the Earth once in 89 minutes and is brought back to Earth safely.

But we are talking opera here, and of those, there are only two and a half. *Oedipus rex* (1927) is more oratorio, so it doesn't count, fascinating though it is for its deliberately non-dramatic presentation of the most dramatic classical story of all time. *Mavra* (1922) is a tiny *opera buffa*, after a story by Pushkin, and is satirical in its homage to Stravinsky's Russian forebears. Wicked or what?

In fact, Stravinsky wrote only one full-length opera. *The Rake's Progress* was first staged in 1951 and is a sort of baroque opera in shape and attitude, the music equally formal and objective, but refracted, disjointed, angular, as befits its eighteenth-century story after William Hogarth's series of allegorical pictures. Tom Rakewell leaves Anne Trulove and is tempted by Shadow (the Devil in disguise) to marry the fantastic bearded lady Baba the Turk, then to place his trust in a machine for turning stones into bread. He reclaims his soul from Shadow, but goes mad and ends up in Bedlam. The libretto was written by W. H. Auden and Chester Kallman.

It's a tough piece to produce (certainly not too short) and in the wrong hands may sound dry, but its sequence of set numbers can be molded into a touching and tragic experience.

Hockney and the Rake

One of the most striking productions of *The Rake's Progress* was that designed by the British artist David Hockney (b. 1937) for an English production of 1975. It's not too often that a painter gets a chance to make, as it were, a bigger splash than normal, with a large, three-dimensional stage as his canvas. Hockney seized the chance with both hands, paying homage to Hogarth's original series of engravings with his own use of line and hatch, and equally paying homage to Stravinsky's neo-classical outlook with his series of contradictory perspectives. There is just one problem, with this and other Hockney designs: they are sometimes just so good that you forget about the drama and music they are supposed to embrace.

LEFT Smashing cop-show version of the *Rake* staged by the Théâtre du Chatelet in Paris, 1996.

1912 Britons have a miserable time, with a coal strike, a dock strike, and a transport workers' strike.

1922 Lawrence of Arabia withdraws from public duty and, joins the British Royal Air Force under the name of John Hume Ross; when his identity is discovered, he transfers to the Royal Tank Corps as T.E. Shaw.

1931 London's new Sadler's Wells Theatre opens under the management of Lilian Baylis on 6 January.

1910~1980

The Outsiders

Britten and *Peter Grimes*

ABOVE The sea and the men who work with it form the backdrop to many of Britten's operas.

What had happened meanwhile to opera in the United Kingdom? Well, there had been some operatic activity – Ethel Smyth's patchy The Wreckers *(1906), Ralph Vaughan Williams'* Sir John in Love *(1928) and* Riders to the Sea *(1932), Rutland Boughton's Wagnerian* The Immortal Hour *(1914). But on the whole there was not much of startling significance until the young(ish) Benjamin* BRITTEN *(1913–76) burst onto the scene with* Peter Grimes, *first given on a historic night – 7 June 1945 to be precise – at Sadler's Wells Theatre in London. What was so important about* Grimes *was that it was strikingly individual – new, confident, immediately resonant. Its story, about an outcast fisherman in Britten's adopted home town of Aldeburgh, on the bleak British east coast, is sinister and pursues themes that were to obsess Britten until he died. It's captivating stuff, full of sea-sounds.*

Britten's heroes reflect aspects of his own personality. He was gay and living with his partner, the tenor *Peter* PEARS (b. 1910), when it was not the done thing – illegal, in fact, in the U.K. Thus he himself was the outsider. He was also obsessed with young boys, as was Grimes (who is alleged to have murdered his own apprentice) – though Britten's obsession seems to have been fairly harmless. His music is soaked in themes of innocence and experience, and

RIGHT Benjamin Britten seated at the piano with Peter Pears (holding sheet music), who created the title role of Peter Grimes and many other of Britten's operas.

1948 Following a tradition of giving them spirits' names from Shakespeare's plays, Uranus's fifth satellite is called Miranda, after the heroine of *The Tempest*.

1960 The first weather satellites are launched, bringing prior warning of hurricanes and storms and thereby saving lives.

1978 British author Iris Murdoch writes her novel *The Sea, The Sea*.

ABOVE Jon Vickers and Heather Harper in the 1984 production of *Peter Grimes* by Elijah Moshinsky.

Aldeburgh Festival

Opera composers have one constant problem: where are their operas going to be staged? Britten solved that one for himself when, in 1948, he and his partner Peter Pears began the Aldeburgh Festival in East Suffolk, England, where they lived. At first, the English Opera Group, which Britten and Pears helped to found, was responsible for artistic direction. Productions took place in the tiny Jubilee Hall until Snape Maltings, a few miles inland, was converted into a versatile concert hall in 1967. The Festival hosted the premieres of Britten's *A Midsummer Night's Dream, Death in Venice*, the children's pieces *Let's Make an Opera* (1949) and *Noye's Fludde* (1958), and all three church parables – highly stylized dramas influenced by Japanese Noh theater. Not a bad record for a remote fishing village.

Ethel Smyth (1858–1944)

Dame Ethel Smyth was the suffragette of music in Britain. By all accounts a formidably wilful woman, she bucked trends by going off to Leipzig to study. Brahms, Grieg, Tchaikovsky, and Dvorák all took her very seriously, and with good reason. Her operas include *Fantasio* (1898), which, though a success, she came to disapprove of, burning all the scores she could lay her hands on in 1916. There followed *Der Wald* (1902) – seen in Berlin, the Met in New York, and at Covent Garden, London – and *The Wreckers*, set in an eighteenth-century Cornish village that survives by luring ships onto the rocky coast, which established itself in British pre-war repertoire. Smyth's work is uneven, but at its best it occasionally bears comparison with Wagner in its full-blooded Romanticism.

the threat of tainting purity. *Billy Budd* (1951), the claustrophobic *The Turn of the Screw* (1954), the pacifistic *Owen Wingrave* (1970), and above all, *Death in Venice* (1973) incorporate these elements.

But if you want sheer magic, turn to *A Midsummer Night's Dream* (1960). No composer has ever evoked the nocturnal, slightly sinister magic of Shakespeare's play more exquisitely.

1904 In New York a woman is arrested for smoking a cigarette in public.

1906 The Manhattan Opera Company is formed by Oscar Hammerstein – in its four seasons it will be so successful as to threaten the Metropolitan Opera, which offers Hammerstein $1,200,000 to refrain from producing opera in New York for 10 years. He agrees.

1913 Everyone's doing the Charleston (and Black Bottom), as the foxtrot rages in ballrooms worldwide.

1900~1950
Opera U.S.A.
Finding an Identity

Britten gained much of the confidence to write Grimes *from his visit to the United States at the beginning of World War II. But what was happening in opera there? Good question. For the first American opera we have to go back to William Henry* FRY*'s* Leonora *of 1845 and George Frederick* BRISTOW*'s* Rip Van Winkle *a decade later (no sleeping in the theater now, please). There were many successors, but they were hardly native in style, and whatever successful opera there was tended to be of the imported European variety.*

BELOW *Porgy and Bess* with Willard White and Cynthia Haymon; the opera was based on a play, *Porgy*, by Du Bose and Dorothy Heyward.

Establishing a national identity was the main problem for American artists in general, and it wasn't until the twentieth century that American opera really came into its own. Initially, there were pieces like *Frederick Shepherd* CONVERSE*'s The Pipe of Desire* (1906), the first American work given at the Metropolitan Opera in New York. Later there were efforts to create a Native American opera – in 1916, *Paul Hastings* ALLEN*'s The Last of the Mohicans* was even performed in Italian

in Florence. But it was only with works like *George* GERSHWIN*'s Porgy and Bess* (1935) – a masterpiece of invention and orchestration by any standards – *Virgil* THOMSON*'s* boldly experimental *Four Saints in Three Acts* (1934, to a libretto by Gertrude Stein, and a sort of proto-minimalist opera), and *The Mother of Us All* (1947) that American opera could claim an identity all its own.

Later composers, like *Douglas* MOORE (1893–1969), *Carlisle* FLOYD (b. 1926),

1919 In Norfolk, Virginia, the first dial telephones appear on the scene.

1935 In the U.S. the electric Hammond Organ, with two manuals and a pedal keyboard, becomes popular.

1952 The first tranquillizers using the drug reserpine, obtained from the root of an Indian shrub, are launched on an unsuspecting world.

and *Robert WARD* (b. 1917) have made their own individual, if relatively conservative, marks. Floyd's *Susannah* (1955) and Ward's *The Crucible* (1961) are both popular in the United States, but haven't traveled much, if at all. Perhaps the most successful American opera composer is *Gian Carlo MENOTTI* (born in Italy in 1911, but long an American resident, although he now lives in a castle in Scotland). His post-*verismo* pieces include *The Telephone* (1947, with a cast of one), *The Medium* (1946), *The Consul* (1950, dealing with the plight of refugees), and *Amahl and the Night Visitors* (1951).

Menotti

Partner of Samuel Barber, founder of the Spoleto Festival of Two Worlds, librettist for Barber's *Vanessa* (1958), Menotti's most famous works are given in the main text, particularly *Amahl and the Night Visitors*, which was written for television. Later pieces tend to be directed toward children, both as subjects and performers. Such pieces include *The Egg* (1976), *Chip and his Dog* (1979), and *The Boy Who Grew Too Fast* (1982). Tunes mean a lot, and Menotti has steadfastly refused to kowtow to the charges of those who would label him a reactionary or conservative in those respects. Good for him! In 1973 Menotti moved to Scotland with his adopted son.

Patrons

Difficult subject – opera needs patrons. Who should they be? The City? The State? Big Business? Rich individuals? In Europe, many houses are supported by a combination of these, State subsidy being seen as somehow immoral. In the U.S., funding is entirely by private contribution, which raises an obvious problem. If you're going to donate a few thousand (or million) dollars to your local opera company, you aren't going to be happy if they produce operas you don't like. And most people are terrified by what they don't know – particularly if it's new and challenging. Result: conservative programming or no opera company. Which is no use for people like us (you are on my side, aren't you?), who want to see as many different operas as possible.

RIGHT Menotti's *Amahl and the Night Visitors*, the first opera written for television. James Rainbird is the boy hero.

1955 Albert Einstein dies, after trying by means of his unified field theory to establish a merger between quantum theory and his general theory of relativity.

1957 The first pacemaker small enough to be inserted under the skin, and not carried around externally, is invented by American physician Clarence Lillehei.

1971 Henry Kissinger visits China secretly to arrange Nixon's visit there.

1950~1990
Through a Glass Darkly
Proliferation and Minimalism

ABOVE Opera in the U.S.A.; a rare treat.

Getting your opera performed in the United States is difficult. Considering the country's size, opera companies willing to tackle the new are few and far between, though there are honorable exceptions – Houston Grand Opera, for instance. But I wouldn't want to give the impression that composers in the U.S. are slacking. In fact, much the reverse is true. Probably the most popular comtemporary genre of opera in the United States today is that commonly known as minimalist, although there are several sub-species.

The most mesmeric work (or repetitive and dull, according to your point of view) is that by *Philip Glass* (b. 1937), whose operas go under titles like *Einstein on the Beach* (1975), or *Akhnaten* (1984), or *Satyagraha* (1980), or *The Making of the Representative from Planet 8* (1988). It's all very New Age, and very, very slick. And if you suspect I'm using these terms as something other than praise, then you may well be right, though I'll admit that the music benefits from the

RIGHT Egyptian minimalism in *Akhnaten* by Philip Glass, with Sally Burgess as Nefertiti and Christopher Robson as Akhnaten.

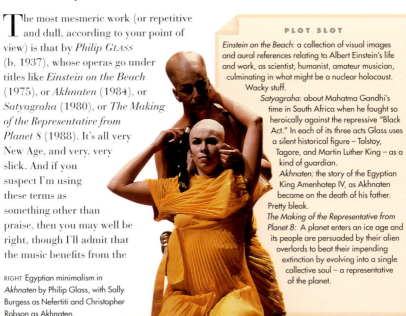

> ### PLOT SLOT
>
> *Einstein on the Beach*: a collection of visual images and aural references relating to Albert Einstein's life and work, as scientist, humanist, amateur musician, culminating in what might be a nuclear holocaust. Wacky stuff.
>
> *Satyagraha*: about Mahatma Gandhi's time in South Africa when he fought so heroically against the repressive "Black Act." In each of its three acts Glass uses a silent historical figure – Tolstoy, Tagore, and Martin Luther King – as a kind of guardian.
>
> *Akhnaten*: the story of the Egyptian King Amenhotep IV, as Akhnaten became on the death of his father. Pretty bleak.
>
> *The Making of the Representative from Planet 8:* A planet enters an ice age and its people are persuaded by their alien overlords to beat their impending extinction by evolving into a single collective soul – a representative of the planet.

1985 An American passenger on the *Achille Lauro* cruise liner is killed when 450 hostages are seized by Palestinian hijackers, before they eventually give themselves up and are jailed.

1988 Radiocarbon dating proves that the Shroud of Turin was made thirteen centuries too late to have been the shroud of Jesus.

1990 American composer/conductor Leonard Bernstein dies, having updated the Romeo and Juliet story in his enormously successful *West Side Story*.

TO NOTE ~ **NAMES**

Many American composers have taken the bit between their teeth: **George Antheil** *(1900–59) with* Transatlantic *in 1930;* **Bernard Herrmann** *(1911–75) with* Wuthering Heights *in 1951;* **Aaron Copland** *(1900–90) with* The Tender Land *in 1954;* **Ned Rorem** *(b. 1923) with* The Robbers *in 1958 and* Miss Julie *in 1965;* **Samuel Barber** *(b. 1910) with* Vanessa *in 1958 and* Antony and Cleopatra *in 1966;* **Roger Sessions** *(1896–1985) with* Montezuma *in 1964; and so on and so forth, until – and beyond –* **John Corigliano's** The Ghost of Versailles *in 1991: the first work to be commissioned and performed by the Met since the opening of the Lincoln Center.*

NAMES ~ **TO NOTE**

spectacular stagings that these pieces have received. And that I'm probably in a minority.

Then there's *John ADAMS* (b. 1947), who makes real substance out of pattern in his user-friendly music. His operas have topical themes: *Nixon in China* (1987) is about – well, Nixon in China. *The Death of Klinghoffer* (1991), less obviously, is about the hijacking of the *Achille Lauro* and its tragic consequences in 1985.

BELOW *The Making of The Representative from Planet 8 in the English National Opera production.*

What is Minimalism?

I could leave a blank space to make the point. Or I could be nasty and say that minimalism is music that expands to fill a space, rather than music that creates its own space. Or I could be kind and say that it's music whose repetitive nature takes the consciousness to a different, higher spiritual plane. No help? Okay. Minimalism is a term coined by British composer Michael Nyman, and it's generally taken to refer to music that relies on repeated, slowly metamorphosing patterns, for better or worse, louder or quieter, faster or slower. It works best when the piece is short and modest in other respects, if you ask me – Steve Reich's *Music for Pieces of Wood*, for instance – but others who champion the works of, say, Philip Glass would disagree.

1928 At Fleetwood in England, a machine for boning and cleaning kippers is given its inaugural run.

1932 Eric Gill sculpts "Prospero and Ariel," his second most famous piece, for the B.B.C.'s Broadcasting House London.

1943 As lindy hop gives way to jitterbugging zoot suits become *the* mode of the day among American hepcats.

1920~1990

What's It All About?
Berio and Structuralism

What is opera? Come to that, what is drama? What is music? What, even, is singing? The answers to these questions can't be found in the work of the Italian composer Luciano BERIO (b. 1925). But you can at least find the questions and some stimulating food for thought for heated, early-hours debate. It's exquisite music, though you need to be pretty well informed if you are to catch all its allusions.

Italo Calvino (1923–87)
Born in Cuba of Italian parents, Calvino used his experience of fighting with the Partisans against the Nazis in his first, "neo-realist" novel, *The Path to the Nest of Spiders* (1947). Thereafter, he became interested in expanding the limits of realism by exploring fantasy and myth in three allegorical novels entitled *Our Ancestors,* and in depicting the fabulous realms in novels such as *Invisible Cities* (1972). His later works were profound and complex, combining great inventiveness with hard, satirical wit.

His operatic output – and all his music, sung or played, is by definition dramatic – began with *Passaggio* in 1963. Avant-garde though it was, *Passaggio* was, however, only a beginning. Afterward came an opera called *Opera* (1970), which interweaves three different kinds of theater on the common theme of death. Opera in this context means simply "works," in the plural. It's complex stuff, with lots of breakings off, reworkings, resumptions. There are parts from Alessandro Striggio's libretto for *Orfeo,* sections from a play about the treatment of the terminally ill, and parts from a project that Berio had earlier undertaken about the sinking of the *Titanic.* Ambitious isn't the word!

RIGHT *Un re in Ascolto,* a spectacular Berio/Calvino collaboration.

1954 Two inventions in one year – the contraceptive pill and plastic contact lenses – revolutionize the lives of millions of users.

1980 The wreck of the *Titanic* is located in the Atlantic Ocean, 12,000 feet down.

1991 During the six-week Gulf War following the invasion of Kuwait by Iran, two British airmen are shot down and tortured.

UNITY AND FRAGMENTATION

Too ambitious, in fact, and for Berio's next operatic essay, *La vera storia* (1981), he wrote the music before asking Italo Calvino to supply the words. That way the musical unity was guaranteed. And it's an ingenious unity – separate numbers in the first half, a fused reworking in the second half. The same story is re-enacted in contemporary terms, the traditional operatic heroes and villains now anonymous passers-by.

Un re in ascolto (1984), again composed to Calvino's words, is likewise musically unified. Calvino's text came first, but Berio fragmented it to suit the musical whole. And the music itself? Adventurous and beautifully imagined, colorful, and elliptical. Don't expect nineteenth-century-style tunes.

PLOT SLOT

The scenario of *Passaggio* is simple: a woman crosses the stage and stops at various points. But she suggests a powerfully affecting sequence of arrest, torture, and release. There's a chorus in the pit that comments on her plight, and in the audience are groups that give voice to their reactions. Everything to do with the operatic experience is deconstructed, exposed. *Un re in ascolto* is about a theatrical impresario, Prospero, who loses his grip on his domain. The Protagonist, for which he has been auditioning applicants, cannot be possessed or controlled. When she finally appears, he has to confront that fact and, having done so, dies. All the world's a stage…

Italianate Grace

After studies in Milan with the Italian composer Giorgio Ghedini (1892–1965) in the immediate post-war period, Berio went off to Tanglewood (you know, Berkshire Festival, Tanglewood, Mass.) to learn about serialism in the early 1950s with Luigi Dallapiccola (1904–75, and probably the first Italian composer to adopt 12-note methods). Soon Berio became aligned with the powerful Boulez/Stockhausen faction. His music, though intellectually rigorous, is always tempered with a certain Italianate grace and suppleness, and it's not without its wit, either. It is influenced by contemporary linguistic studies, always concerned with the merging of music into language. (Or is it vice versa? Or are they different versions, at different conscious levels, of the same thing?) Piece to try: *Sinfonia* (1969), an undoubted masterpiece of the century – a collage that quotes extracts from Mahler's Second Symphony, Wagner's *Das Rheingold*, Ravel's *La Valse*, Debussy's *La Mer*, and Strauss's *Der Rosenkavalier*.

1931 Nylon rules, as an American chemist Wallace Hume Carothers finds a fabric that is even stronger than silk.

1947 Television sets may show fuzzy pictures and have very few actual programs to offer, but they are finally viable for the general public – home entertainment, advertising, show business, and even politics will never be the same again.

1959 Stockhausen writes *Zyklus* for a solo percussionist, in which the performer may start at any of its seventeen pages and progress backward or forward until the starting point is reached.

1930~2002

Contemporary King
The Renewal of the Epic

BELOW Karlheinz Stockhausen in the early 60s contemplating the future of opera electronica.

Karlheinz STOCKHAUSEN (b. 1928), torch-bearer for the post-1945 German avant-garde and for long renowned as the harbinger of all that's worst about contemporary music – impersonal, long-winded, academic – actually isn't that bad. You certainly can't fault his wacky imagination when the work-list includes pieces written in order to communicate with aliens. If there is a criticism to be made of his music, it is that it becomes a process rather than a drama. But he didn't turn to opera as such until 1977, though in the early 1970s there were works that demanded a certain amount of staging – special lighting, performers in costume, and the rest. Trans *(1971),* Sirius *(1977), and* Atmen gibt das Leben *(1974) are all good instances. The same period saw a change in Stockhausen's compositional technique to something based on tight organization and an exploration of melody:*

When Stockhausen did set about writing an opera, he didn't do it by halves. In fact, he decided to devote the 25 years from 1977 to writing an immense cycle of seven operas, each devoted to a day of the week and collectively called *Licht*. That gives him until the year 2002. He's on target, too. The characters in this unlikely project are suitably biblical-astrological-mythological: Michael and Lucifer, a black cat, Kathinka. Probably to

Stockhausens Junior

As a personality, Stockhausen has acquired something of a reputation for an almost Wagnerian dominance, but he has produced two brilliant musician sons: the trumpeter Markus Stockhausen and the saxophonist Simon Stockhausen, both of whom happily cross boundaries between musical types.

1961 East Germany builds a wall around West Berlin, which reduces the flow of refugees from East to West to a trickle.

1981 Andrew Lloyd Webber's *Cats* makes a surprising musical success of the poems of T.S. Eliot.

1987 A notebook of Mozart's containing symphonies 22–30 is sold at auction for a staggering $4 million.

keep the wolf from the door, each of the operas' premieres is prefaced by a sequence of premieres of other pieces, all of which make up the opera. But seen in the flesh, as it were, Stockhausen's approach does not appear to be piecemeal. These are great spectacles, quirky perhaps (one opera, premiered at La Scala, featured the house's very own strike), but magnificent nevertheless, with the Master himself controlling every aspect of production, much

Stockhausen's Life and Times

In 1951, Stockhausen attended the Darmstadt summer-school courses and became hooked on the notion of serialism being applied to rhythm as well as pitch. He then composed a number of pieces that explored such avenues – fascinating or severe, according to taste (and probably mood). He also pioneered electronic music, with two *Studies* written in 1954; mixed free and strict tempos in *Zeitmasze* (1956); in *Gesang der Jünglinge* (1956) combined live and recorded sounds and invented what became known in the late 1980s' hi-tech pop world as "sampling"; and in *Aus dem sieben Tagen* (1968) merely instructed the musician to play whatever comes into his mind while reading and meditating on Stockhausen's prose-poems.

RIGHT Mama said there'd be days like this: *Donnerstag* (Thursday) from Stockhausen's *Licht*.

PLOT SLOT

Licht (light) isn't so much an opera with a plot as an opera made up of a set of quasi-religious rituals. Stockhausen's biographer Michael Kurtz has put it like this: *Licht* is "an attempt to create a cosmic World theater which summarizes and intensifies [Stockhausen's] lifelong concern: the unity of music and religion, allied to the vision of an essentially musical mankind." The three main characters are Eve, Lucifer, and the archangel Michael, but this isn't just an ordinary biblical story. If anything, it's supposed to be the new bible of some space-age super-religion. As with all religions, either you swallow it or you don't. And Stockhausen (who now publishes his own music, in score and on CD) has made a habit of fashioning constituent parts of these highly integrated wholes as free-standing pieces – neat marketing idea.

as his great forebear Wagner did at Bayreuth. Indeed, *Licht* is a kind of cosmic *Ring*, though perhaps its sense of ceremonial makes it closer to *Parsifal*. Audacious, but worth seeing and hearing, though productions don't crop up every other week.

1931 The two-millionth British telephone is accepted by King George V for use at Buckingham Palace.

1945 In Budapest, Raoul Wallenberg, who has saved the lives of countless Hungarian Jews, disappears.

1966 America has 78 million cars and 16 million trucks and buses fighting for space on its roads – and things can only get worse...

1930~1990

Adventures in Opera
Ligeti and the Macabre

Like Berio, György LIGETI (b.1923) explores drama in every musical situation. Anyone who wants a condensed example of how he does it should listen to his Aventures *(1962), in which voices engage in a complex counterpoint of exaggerated vocal gestures using nonsense syllables – funny, brilliant, and saying something about the way human beings express their feelings. There was the possibility of a comic-strip opera* Oedipus, *but the librettist Goeran GENTELE (1917–72) died before it had progressed very far.*

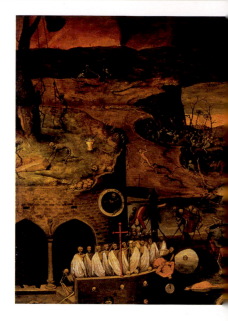

Micropolyphony

This is Ligeti's favorite textural device. What happens is simple in concept: you put so many different strands of music together that the ear becomes confused and can distinguish individual lines only with great difficulty. What is created is, in effect, an ever-evolving but single texture, out of which might emerge a splash of this, a hint of that. The most basic visual equivalent might be a painting of alternating black and white horizontal lines. If you paint them thinly or stand back, the effect turns into a single mass of grey – only in the case of micropolyphony, there are many more colors and thicknesses. It's the opposite of polyphony, where the point is to hear all the lines at once, if you can.

Then in 1977 Ligeti completed *Le Grand Macabre*, after a play by Michel de Ghelderode. It's a weird examination of the human condition, ranging from sex, politics, and drunkenness to, of course, death, and set in the kingdom of Breughel's landscapes. The overture is for 12 motor horns, and that gives a general indication of the opera's flavor, its winning decrepitude. Whether or not Nekrotzar, the Great Macabre himself, means it when he announces the end of the world is unclear. What is plain is Ligeti's marvelous gift for taking a look at life and death from another, bizarre, hugely entertaining angle.

1971 William G. Wilson, founder of Alcoholics Anonymous in 1935, dies.

1979 Punk-rock singer Sid Vicious meets a vicious end in a drug overdose.

1989 After an emotional visit to Moscow in 1986, where he performed to a rapturous Russian reception, pianist Vladimir Horowitz dies in America, his adopted country.

Ligeti's Life and Times

Ligeti was born in the Hungarian part of Transylvania (and there is something distinctly of the mad scientist about his appearance), studied and taught in Budapest, but early on

ABOVE Ligeti's metronome choir.

in his composing career began moving away from the nationalistic influences of Bartók. He emigrated after the Hungarian Uprising of 1956 and settled in Cologne, Germany, where he worked at the electronic music studio. His music is a combination of ultra-refined, often massive textures and the kind of wit – funny on the surface but exposing an inner seriousness (his *Poème symphonique* is scored for 100 metronames) – that makes you view things from different, newly revealing angles. Most famous pieces: *Lux aeterna* (1966) and the organ work *Volumina* (1962), which was for once appropriately appropriated for a film, Stanley Kubrick's *2001: A Space Odyssey* – but not the "great dawning" music: that is Richard Strauss's *Also sprach Zarathustra* of 1896.

ABOVE One of Brueghel the Elder's characteristic works, *The Triumph of Death* (c.1560), a fit setting for Ligeti's *Grand Macabre*.

What more encouragement do you need? Okay, then, what about the second scene, when Astrodamors and Mescalina copulate, he clad in women's underwear (over his trousers), she in leather, brandishing a whip, before he falls asleep and she demands a lover who is more generously proportioned in the genitalia department. And you thought opera was staid!

LEFT *Le Grand Macabre* in a 1982 staging; Mescalina (what a name!) is obviously too much of a woman for Astrodamors to handle.

121

1928 Mickey Mouse, in characteristic white gloves and with black ears, is created and makes his film debut in *Plane Crazy*.

1942 "The White Cliffs of Dover" and "White Christmas" capture the spirit of the moment.

1974 In America, "streaking" becomes the latest fad of the moment.

1930~1995
Respecting Tradition
Hans Werner Henze

After World War II, the German composer Hans Werner HENZE (b. 1926) had dealings with the avant-garde group that included Stockhausen, but his heart didn't really lie there. He was always more of a traditionalist. That doesn't mean, however, that he writes in an old style; merely that he sees his operas as continuing an evolutionary line. They reinterpret old forms, often quite brilliantly. Henze has always been a man of the theater. He first made his living as a répétiteur, after studying at the Brunswick State Music School in Heidelberg and privately with the German composer and teacher Wolfgang Fortner (b. 1907) from 1946 until 1948.

ABOVE Hans Werner Henze as a young man; following a well-established tradition among composers, he left Germany (in 1953) to settle in Italy.

Manon's Story
The basis of the Manon story was Abbé Prévost's *Manon Lescaut*: the Chevalier Des Grieux falls in love and elopes with Manon, only for her to desert him, then die in his arms at the end. The major difference between Puccini's *Manon Lescaut* and Henze's *Boulevard Solitude* was Henze's shifting of the focus from Manon to Armand Des Grieux. Henze's opera ends in a fast "revue," with images from their life together seen over the sounds of a children's choir.

His first opera, *Boulevard Solitude*, was composed in 1951, and made an immediate impression with its reinterpretation of the Manon story. He used Schoenberg's 12-note system, but integrated it with dance, drama, and cinematic as well as nineteenth-century operatic forms. Two radio operas and a huge reputation soon followed, but Henze became disillusioned with Germany and moved to Italy in 1953. His second opera, *König Hirsch* (1956), was a mammoth five-hour affair and, as if to make a point, used a freer, altogether more luxuriant language. Subsequently, opera became the most important genre in Henze's output.

1986 Whitney Houston and Madonna are the new divas of popular music.

1989 The Berlin Wall comes crashing down, as East German refugees stream to the West and the communist government collapses.

1994 Traditional Irish dancing in a contemporary mode hits the world, as Irish phenomenon Riverdance take to the stage.

PLOT SLOT

Henze's masterpiece, *The Bassarids*, is based on Euripides' *The Bacchae*, first performed in 405 B.C. Here's the story: Pentheus, King of Thebes, falls under the spell of the god Dionysius, despite forbidding worship of him. Eventually, Pentheus is torn to pieces by Dionysiac worshippers led by his mother Agave in a trance, after the people of Thebes have been transformed into Bassarids and Maenads. Emerging from her frenzy, Agave realizes what she has done, as Dionysius summons his mother Semele and translates her to Mount Olympus as the goddess Thyone, at whose vine-covered grave the people now worship.

ABOVE The Olympian lovers, Venus and Adonis (Henry Regnault, 1810), a traditional inspiration for one of Henze's most gorgeous operas.

TO NOTE · NAMES

Henze *based* Der Prinz von Homburg *(1960) on nineteenth-century Italian opera (Bellini and Verdi especially);* Elegy for Young Lovers *(1961) is a ravishingly beautiful opera of short scenes;* Der junge Lord *(1965) is an* opera buffa *modeled on Rossini;* The Bassarids *(1966), arguably his operatic masterpiece, is also a four-movement symphony.*

POLITICO-SOCIAL COMMENT

After *The Bassarids*, Henze explored the political and social possibilities of music drama, and when he came back to opera, with *We Come to the River* (1976, a work in two parts and 11 scenes), he showed the influence of a more gestural, less self-consciously constructed music. Thereafter, he rediscovered his natural lyricism: in *The English Cat* (1983) – a politico-social satire – in the Berglike *Das verratene Meer* (1990), and most recently in the lovely madrigal and bolero sequence of *Venus und Adonis* (1997), which is full of ravishing sounds. It just goes to show that if you are an opera, you don't have to be a century old to be beautiful.

1906 Soprano Geraldine Farrar makes her debut in America – she will go on to sing at the Metropolitan Opera House in New York nearly 500 times in 29 different roles.

1925 New York experiences its first solar eclipse in three hundred years.

1968 Space exploration really takes off, with *Apollos 7* and *8* launched and successfully splashing down in the Atlantic after achieving their orbits.

1900~1980

Light and Dark, Good and Evil
Michael Tippett

*The British composer Sir Michael T*IPPETT *(1905–98) lived to be a grand old man, but his spirit remained famously young. He grew up very much in Britten's shadow, yet, once the Musical Establishment accepted him as a different kind of composer, he showed that he was just as inventive and imaginative, and perhaps more innovative, than his younger compatriot.*

ABOVE Yin/yang in opera: Tippett's forte.

There was an early ballad opera, *The Village Opera* (1928), based largely on an eighteenth-century piece, and a folksong opera called *Robin Hood* in 1934 (libretto by "D. M. Pennyless"); but Tippett's entrée into the operatic world really came with *The Midsummer Marriage*, completed in 1952 (like its successors, to Tippett's own libretto) and first seen in 1955. It's a visionary piece. The music glows, but is also strong-limbed, even masculine in its counterpoint. The work idealizes the human relationship through spiritual and psychic unity. You might say it's about the sixth sense through which we communicate and experience bonding one with another.

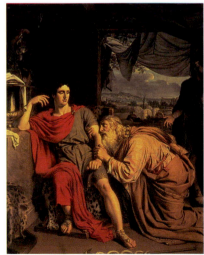

ABOVE The Trojan king Priam begs for the body of his son Hector from the Greek hero Achilles, who has killed Hector in a one-on-one duel amid the ruins of Troy (Alexander Ivanov, 1824).

1971 The first portable calculator goes on sale, weighing 2½lbs and costing $150.

1980 On January 1, Kew Gardens in London raises its entrance fee from 1 penny to 10 pence – inflation, or what?

1990 Mikhail Gorbachev is awarded the Nobel Peace Prize for his efforts to defuse East–West tensions.

LEFT Alexander Malta as the distraught Priam in the Royal Opera's stark 1985 staging.

THE SEARCH FOR SELF AND FOR PARADISE

After this wonderful piece, *King Priam* (1962) seemed to represent a change of direction. Now Tippett's music was lean, relying on colliding, fragmented sounds, as befitted the brutal story of the fall of Troy (see also Berlioz). Even so there are beautiful moments – Achilles' song, sung to his friend Patroclus – and the opera is as powerful as any Tippett has written. So is *The Knot Garden* (1970), a dense, fast-moving score about the turmoil of human relationships and how they change and are resolved. This work, by the way, includes the first openly gay character in opera, the musician Dov. *The Ice Break* (1977) projects these themes into the realms of race and parenthood, a search for paradise on Earth, which can only come as a job-lot with the bitterness of experience. Finally, *New Year* (1988), an exploration, complete with visitors from outer space, of Jo Ann's attempts to find herself, and as youthful, dynamic, and eclectic a score – there is even rap in it – as Tippett ever wrote. All of Tippett's operas direct themselves to one kind of enlightenment or another. They chart an extraordinary stylistic passage, testifying to their composer's willingness always to risk something new.

The Fall of Troy

The fall of the city of Troy, after being besieged by the Greeks in the thirteenth century B.C., formed the mainstay of Homer's epic poem, the *Iliad*. Tippet takes up Homer's theme of the wrath of the Greek hero Achilles at the death of his friend Patroclus, and Achilles' murder of Hector, son of the Trojan King Priam. The opera ends with the killing of King Priam before the altar by Achilles' son.

Tippett's Life and Times

Sir Michael Tippett studied composition at London's Royal College of Music in the 1920s, when its reputation for stuffiness (separate staircases for male and female students) was probably at its height. He didn't write what he considered his first worthwhile piece, the Concerto for Double String Orchestra, until his thirties. His kind of music was very different: contrapuntal, luminous in texture, rich in harmony, tough, vital, and tautly sprung. Politically, he was also a rebel and spent six months in prison for refusing to contribute even in non-military duties toward the war effort. His powerful *A Child of Our Time* (1941) asks that hatred and oppression be condemned, but recognizes the dark and light sides of human nature.

1948 The song "All I Want for Christmas is My Two Front Teeth" becomes popular.

1956 Barbara Hepworth produces her sculpture of Orpheus.

1967 Birtwistle and Maxwell Davies found the Pierrot Players, named after Schoenberg's melodrama *Pierrot lunaire*, for the performance of new chamber music involving theatrical elements. In 1970 it is reorganized as The Fires of London.

1940~1990

Myth and Morality
Birtwistle and Maxwell Davies

These two knights of the realm, both hailing from the northwest of England, both the same age, have for more than 30 years carried the burden of notoriety upon their shoulders. Neither would admit to radicalism; the fact is that both Birtwistle and Maxwell Davies possess hugely original minds and have an untameable instinct for the process of inventing music. Both demand that their listeners' minds are open and alert. For them, easy listening is not listening at all, and I have to agree with that. But there the similarities cease.

ABOVE *The Mask of Orpheus* staged literally, with masks (1986).

ABOVE Birtwistle's *Punch and Judy*, chic, sinister, and violent.

Harrison BIRTWISTLE (b.1934), with a reputation for being awkward and bluff (he's actually a kinder person than that), has composed several operatic masterpieces and a good deal of what might be called music theater besides. It's difficult to be witty and light-hearted about what he does, because it's all deadly serious – even when it's funny. *Punch and Judy* (1968) turns the traditional English children's show into a piece of disturbing, stylized violence contained within elegant forms; *Down by the Greenwood Side*, a "dramatic pastoral" (1969, to a libretto by Michael Nyman – see pp.132–3), uses old folk-tales to make a ritual of interleaved comedy and tragedy, speech and music.

Then Birtwistle undertook a momentous project, the *Mask of Orpheus*, composed in two batches (1973–6 and 1981–4). (The Royal Opera got bored with waiting, but the rival English National Opera rescued the piece from incompletion and oblivion.) It is a magical, extended ritual that looks at its subject from the perspective of different viewpoints, with a score that holds one spellbound. It was succeeded by another folk-derived piece, *Yan Tan Tethera* (1986), and then by *Gawain* (1991), a re-telling of the medieval English text *Sir Gawain and the Green Knight* and an enormous, enthralling achievement by any standards.

1970 The amount of British money that its citizens can take abroad is upped from £50 to £300.

1977 The King of rock 'n' roll, Elvis Presley, dies of a drug overdose.

1986 In Bournemouth, England, an unknown score by Edward Elgar is unexpectedly discovered in a drawer.

KINETIC MUSIC

Birtwistle's predilection for ritual is reflected in the processional nature of much of his work. The unstoppably prolific *Peter MAXWELL DAVIES* (b. 1934), on the other hand, is a composer of "kinetic" music, much of it inspired by the wild seascape near his Scottish retreat on the island of Hoy. But his structures are often equally highly ritualized, involving such arcane matters as magic squares (whatever they might be). Proportion's the thing. It is his large-scale pieces, *Taverner* (1968) – based on the life of the sixteenth-century

ABOVE The inspirational island of Hoy.

English composer of that name, but really about issues like integrity and (a favorite subject) betrayal – and the long-gestated,

> ### NAMES TO NOTE
>
> **Maxwell Davies** *has also cultivated the genre of music theater, causing scandal with* Eight Songs for a Mad King *(1969) and with* Miss Donnithorne's Maggot *(1974), both to texts by Randolph Stow. There are also the masques* Blind Man's Buff *(1972),* Le Jongleur de Notre Dame *(1978),* Songs of Hoy *(1982), and a piece with the unlikely title of* The No. 11 Bus *(1984). The chamber opera* The Lighthouse *(1980) is a haunting mystery.*

bizarre, and complex *Resurrection* (1988) that are his most impressive operatic achievements. The latter, ostensibly set in a northern working-class home, is about larger things, like the dangers of a materialistic society and the ramifications of social repression, the boy anti-hero becoming a Hitler-figure.

Orpheus Again

Birtwistle's angle on the Orpheus myth is brilliantly original. He rejects a linear, goal-oriented approach. Instead, he presents various episodes surrounding the core myth in parallel, and includes six electronic interludes. There's a lot of interfolding, plus repetitions from different perspectives – multi-layered isn't an adequate description.

RIGHT World premiere (in Cardiff, 1996) of *The Doctor of Myddfai* by Peter Maxwell Davies.

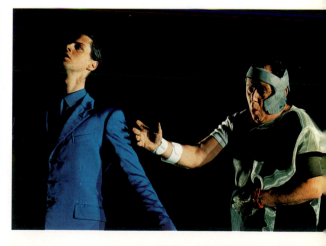

1914 The Calmette-Caillaux affair rocks France: second wife of French politician Joseph Caillaux kills Gaston Calmette, editor of *Le Figaro*, but is acquitted.

1923 In Manhattan, Maria Anna Cecilia Sofia Kalogeropoulous is born – as the rather more pronounceable Maria Callas, she will go on to earn the title *la divina*.

1944 Oceanographer Jacques-Yves Cousteau invents the aqualung and the new sport of scuba diving (= "Self-Contained Underwater Breathing Apparatus") is born.

1914~1990

An Act of Faith
Messiaen and the Birds

ABOVE Messiaen at the keyboard. Composer, organist, and teacher, he numbered Stockhausen (surprisingly) among his pupils.

Some composers, like Verdi, were born to write operas. Others, like Bach, were not. The French composer Olivier MESSIAEN *(1908–92) might be thought of as one of the Bach school. Like Bach, he was a spiritual kind of person, writing works with titles like* Et exspecto resurrectionem mortuorum *(1964). Unlike Bach, he also wrote a number of pieces, such as the* Turangalîla-symphonie *(1949), that glorified – let's put it delicately – the senses. His music came in ritualized blocks, with a style all its own but owing a lot to Eastern cultures. Not the most promising material for the essentially dynamic form of opera.*

But an opera he did write, and it turned out to be an immense one in every respect. Its subject? Well, the clue lay not only in his spirituality, but in another aspect of Messiaen's work, his obsession with birdsong – he'd often go somewhere where birds congregated and carefully notate their calls for later use as decorative themes in his work. So what about an opera on the patron saint of animals, St. Francis? The opera was duly composed to Messiaen's own libretto, taking eight years

Messiaen's Faith

Messiaen was stylistically a composer very much out on his own. His biggest asset was his strongly held Catholic faith, which lent his music – however simple and naïve it seemed on the outside – an inner certitude and spiritual strength. But for Messiaen, the sensual aspects of life were also part and parcel of God's inheritance, a stance reflected in many pieces, including a trilogy on the Tristan legend. In the 1950s, he experimented with serialism, extending its principles to rhythm, dynamic, and instrumentation, but soon turned instead to birdsong as a major source of inspiration. He also taught, and his acceptance of any style as long as it was meant (and heard in the inner ear) has had a profound influence on the kaleidoscopic range of music being written today.

ABOVE Nature's own opera, the dawn chorus.

1968 Han Suyin writes *Birdless Summer*, but birdsong has played a major part in Messaien's work – in his youth, he classified the songs of all French birds by region.

1975 In New York, Sarah Caldwell becomes the first woman conductor of the Metropolitan Opera.

1978 Cardinal Karol Wojtyla breaks a 456-year tradition, by becoming the first non-Italian pope, John Paul II, after the demise of his predecessor, who lasted just one month.

Ondes Martenot

The Ondes Martenot is to electronic music what the abacus is to computing: basic, but immensely effective. It is capable of infinite pitch variations – thus it can slide between notes and swoop rapidly from one extreme of the register to another. The shaking action of the finger can produce a tremolo effect that lends a Messiaen melody a degree of sweetness that many find a bit too much. Oh, and it was invented by one Maurice Martenot in 1928. Messiaen wrote for six of the things in his early instrumental work *Fêtes des belles eaux* (1937); André Jolivet (1905–74) wrote a concerto; and Pierre Boulez (b. 1925) even wrote a quartet.

RIGHT Messiaen's great inspiration, St. Francis, preaching to the birds in a panel by Giotto, the chronicler of Assisi.

to complete, from 1975 until 1983, when it was given its first performance in Paris. It's a massive work: a vast chorus of 150 and an almost as vast orchestra of 120, including much percussion and three Ondes Martenot, the electronic instrument whose curious howlings are characteristic of Messiaen's music. Incidentally, his second wife, Yvonne Loriad, is an expert Ondes Martinot player, as well as a fine pianist.

St. Francis is shaped in eight scenes, each a moment in the Saint's life, which do not even try to form a dramatic entity. Naturally, it ends in St. Francis's death, and in a blazing light of resurrection. But it works as an opera of extraordinary visionary confidence, because Messiaen's "blind-faith" techniques enable anything to find a place in the larger, divine order of things.

1945 The first artificial kidney is invented, bringing in a whole new era of artificial organs.

1965 Pirate radio stations, like Radio Caroline, take to the waves from ships anchored off the British coast.

1980 John Lennon is shot dead in New York on the steps of his apartment building.

1940~2000

Taking Risks

Contemporary European Trends

ABOVE Benedict Mason sets the beautiful game to music.

This subject could fill a whole book. Identifying a trend is itself something not to be undertaken lightly, especially when that trend has only just begun. But what can be stated with certainty is that there are several younger European composers taking up the challenge of opera – undismayed by the time it takes, the possibility that the first run (if secured at all) will also be the last, the fact that most opera companies are interested in only the tried-and-trusted audience-pullers and dare not risk all simply to update the repertoire as, say, a theater company might. (Why is it that new plays get so much more attention than new operas ever do?)

BELOW The world's first punk opera, *Greek*, by Mark-Anthony Turnage.

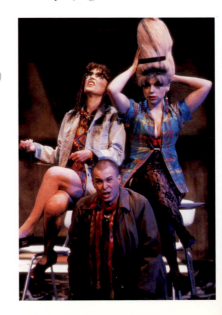

Here are just a few names for starters. In Italy, *Georgio BATISTELLI* (b.1953) has composed deeply original work, stretching the bounds of opera into the beyond with his *Experimentum mundi* (1981, involving a cast of artisans) and *The Cenci* (1997, actors – there are no singers – and instruments hard-wired to computers in this tale of incest and murder). In Germany, thanks in part to operations like the Munich Biennale, founded by Hans Werner Henze, composers such as *Hans-Jürgen VON BOSE* (b.1953) (*63 Dream Palace*, after James Purdy's novel) and *Wolfgang RIHM* (b.1952) have made their marks. England, too, has a clutch of young opera

1984 Band Aid tries to relieve the appalling Ethiopian famine with "Do They Know It's Christmas," which tops the charts worldwide.

1990 Pavarotti lends his weight to soccer's World Cup by taking "Nessun Dorma" to the top of the pop charts.

1997 Hong Kong becomes more Chinese than China itself, as the British hand it back to the People's Republic.

Music Theater

Opera's expensive and productions often fall short of expectations: there's so much to go wrong. Music theater is cheaper, smaller in scale, may require no (or minimal) props, and so is easier to stage. Often it hits home harder. Schoenberg's *Pierrot Lunaire* was one model; others were Stravinsky's *L'histoire du soldat* and *Renard.* Maxwell Davies (see pp.126–7) and Ligeti (see pp.120–1) have been particularly successful in this format. Berio's *Circles* and his sequence of *Sequenzas* for one instrument are also arguably music-theater pieces.

RIGHT *Blond Eckbert* by Judith Weir, with Anne-Marie Owens immured in a fantastical set.

composers, notably *Mark-Anthony Turnage* (b. 1960), who in 1988 set Steven Berkoff's play *Greek* with an alchemic mix of humor and anti-establishment venom (the opera travels widely); but also figures such as *Judith Weir* (b. 1954), whose open, slightly quirky approach has reaped magical results in *A Night at the Chinese Opera* (1987) and *Blond Eckbert* (1994); and *Benedict Mason* (b. 1954), who in his football opera *Playing Away* (1994) incorporates a brilliant, almost Berio-like mixture of stylistic allusions.

Women Composers

Women have historically received short shrift from the music profession, but we shouldn't rewrite history in order to correct past prejudices. Today in Europe there are many female composers doing just as well as their male counterparts, but it's true that large-scale opera seems to be the last bastion that remains to be conquered. I've already mentioned Judith Weir and Ethel Smyth. To them, from Britain, you could add Elizabeth Lutyens (1906–83; best title: *Time off? Not a Ghost of a Chance*, 1971) and Elizabeth Maconchy (b.1907; best title: *The Sofa*, 1967); and from younger generations, Maconchy's daughter Nicola LeFanu (b.1947; her works include the Lorca setting *Blood Wedding*) and Diana Burrell.

1920 Piet Mondrian's *Composition in Red, Yellow and Blue*, with its squares and rectangles of primary colors, gray, and black, has a formative influence on the search for ultimate simplicity in geometric composition.

1952 Composer John Cage produces 4' 33", in which the performer makes no sound, the "music" being the non-silence of the audience.

1969 Pop artist Claes Oldenburg, known for his "soft sculptures" – giant replicas of everyday objects – produces *Lipstick*.

1920~1998

Less Is Even Less
The Minimalist Tendency

ABOVE Opera minimissima.

America has given us some great things, and in the case of opera, as we have seen, they have included some marvelous experimental work by Virgil THOMSON *(1896–1989), which I've labeled proto-minimalism. Minimalism proper, if there is such a thing (and most minimalist composers would deny it), was itself an intriguing angle on art in the 1960s. It brought into the orbit of Western music a touch of the non-occidental, as a reaction to the complexities of Western musical culture, which seemed to have reached a crisis point in the decade before. African music, for instance, is largely based on mesmeric repetition. But as far as I know, there is nothing like an indigenous African operatic form, designed to challenge and charm an audience for three hours. When minimalism is applied on such a large scale, it usually – not always, but usually – falls flat on its face. You can't make something really substantial out of nothing. And you can't – or shouldn't – make music to fill time, but to create its own sense of time.*

Now there are probably hundreds of thousands, millions, even, of people out there who are on the point of taking this book back and claiming a refund. Because minimalist opera, as cultivated by the likes of Philip Glass and John Adams and by the aggressive *Michael* NYMAN (b. 1948, and composer of the soundtrack for Peter Greenaway's films) and the more tender *Gavin* BRYARS (b. 1943) in the U.K., is popular. Glass's *oeuvres* have achieved particular success, and he has a line in neat titles, such as *1000 Airplanes on the Roof* (premiered at Hangar No. 3 at Vienna's International Airport in 1988); there are certainly a lot of them (see p.114). Adams, meanwhile, has tended toward operas on contemporary themes. Generally, he is less of a minimalist in his treatment of ideas than Glass – so much so as to defy even my hard-line definition. As for the English, Nyman's *The Man Who Mistook his Wife for a Hat* (1986, with a libretto after Oliver Sacks' story) has been described as a conjunction between Stravinsky and rock 'n' roll. More of the latter, I would suggest.

1970 Steve Reich writes *Phase Patterns* for four electric organs and, the following year, *Drumming*, for four pairs of turned bongos, three marimbas, three glockenspiels, and male and female voices.

1976 Minimalist sculptor Carl André's *Equivalent VIII*, an arrangement of bricks in Palladian proportion, causes a storm of controversy when it is exhibited at London's Tate Gallery.

1986 Norman Foster builds the dramatic headquarters of the Hong Kong and Shanghai Bank in Hong Kong.

Besides these composers, there are many others who might be called minimalists – the modish Dutchman *Louis ANDRIESSEN* (b. 1939), for one, who applied his aggressive "street-music" style to a highly cultivated structure in *De Materie* (1988). But if you want to find something beyond the glossy, marketable patina of Glass, I guess you will go and find it without my encouragement – or my cautions.

Antipodean Opera

For a country with one of the best-known opera theaters in the world, the Sydney Opera House, Australia's indigenous operatic tradition is alarmingly slight. The first opera written and performed in Australia was *Don John of Austria* (1847), by Isaac Nathan (1790–1864). Since then, it's been a tale of sporadic efforts, by those such as George W. L. Marshall-Hall (1862–1915), a staunch Wagnerian who alarmed audiences in Melbourne; the émigré English composer Fritz Hart (1874–1949: 18 operas in 20 years, mostly unperformed); and Alfred Hill (1870–1960), who co-founded an Australian Opera League. Noted Australian composers Arthur Benjamin (1893–1960) and Malcolm Williamson (b. 1931) wrote operas for London rather than Australia. When George Dreyfus' *Garni Sands* was given in 1972, it was the first professional staging of a full-length Australian opera in its own country since 1904 (Hill's *Tapu*). Music drama on a smaller scale was another matter: works by Barry Conyngham, Gillian Whitehead, Andrew Ford, and others have been given by local groups. Peter Sculthorpe's *Rites of Passage* (1973) was abandoned by Australian Opera when its symbolism baffled audiences, though Richard Meale's *Voss* had a happier reception. There are auditoria with adequate stages and pits, notably in Brisbane and Adelaide, though Perth has refurbished a traditional theater and Melbourne's new State Theater of the Victoria Arts has an impossibly small pit. So work to be done all around, really.

Nyman and Greenaway

Michael Nyman's collaborations with Peter Greenaway have included scores for films *The Draughtsman's Contract, Drowning by Numbers, The Cook, The Thief, His Wife and Her Lover,* and *Prospero's Books.*

LEFT Scene from *Akhnaten* by minimalist maestro Philip Glass.

1990 Deep under the seabed, English and French engineers exchange words, as the two halves of the Channel Tunnel between England and France meet.

1996 The Spice Girls take the pop world by storm – even a bewildered-looking Prince Charles tries to spice up his image by meeting them.

1997 The *Mir* space station spins helplessly out of control – *not* what is meant by going into orbit!

1990~2000

Opera Futura
Things to Come

Whither opera? Who knows? It's survived four centuries, and there's no reason that it should not survive for another four. During its history it has constantly changed – for better or worse, or just plain different. It has spread its tentacles all over the world. It has been austere and extravagant; it has been populist and obscure; it has kowtowed to the mighty and it has provoked them; it has garnished texts with servility and it has exploited them in great washes of musical indulgence.

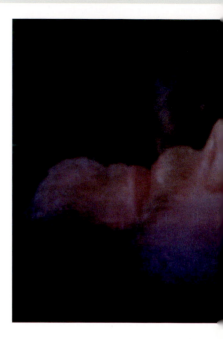

Above all, against all the odds, it has been composed and performed, and never so much as in the twentieth century. And in one shape or another, it will survive for as long as civilization does. People have an unassuageable thirst for the opera theater – it's a place where human feelings are distilled. On one level, it might be necessary to suspend disbelief at all the melodramatic, or magic, heroics and antics going on – and the sight of singers extending their expression of emotion through song is something that you need to get used to. But on another level, opera is hyper-realism.

VIRTUAL OPERA

One thing we can be sure of: new technology will have its say. Already I have witnessed "virtual" scenery, and very effective it was, too. And electronic elements are present in many contemporary scores – in Stockhausen's massive *Licht* cycle, and quite brilliantly in Birtwistle's *Mask of Orpheus*, though, fortunately pointless miking-up is still an operatic rarity. The most significant effect of technology will, however, be in the dissemination of opera. Already we can see and hear many operas in the comfort of our own homes on high-quality videotapes and laser-disc.

1997 In the Nevada desert, *Thrust Supersonic* booms through the sound barrier at a mere 764mph.

1999 The Royal Opera House, Covent Garden, London, shows off its multi-million pound facelift.

2000 The new century comes in with a bang – onstage and off.

LEFT Virtual *Tannhäuser*; Wagner writ even larger than he ever dreamed possible.

Brain Opera

Well, perhaps it's not really an opera, but in my leisure hours I've been wandering around the Internet and have found something called Brain Opera. The idea is that an opera – in the sense of "a work" – is constructed, disseminated and added to on the Internet. There's even a special Internet "hyper-instrument" that appears on-screen to enable you to compose your own sounds, which are then added to the live performances when they happen. It's an intriguing exercise in mass audience participation; so plug in, download the extra bits you need to make it work and turn on. They even let you practice first. Log on. http://www.theremin.media.mit.edu/brainop.html

The advent of the DVD – a compact disc that can store large amounts of video and audio information – will make it even easier to access opera in the home, on the computer, or TV set. Digital radio and television will make live relays more attractive, with all round high fidelity.

GET SURFING

And, of course, there is the Internet, the most powerful communication tool that human beings have yet invented. Once speed of access and band-width problems have been overcome, live Internet hook-ups to any opera house in the world equipped with the right technology will be easy. Can't afford to fly to Timbuktu for that rare Paisiello opera? Get surfing instead. Naturally we can expect such technologies to have their price. Indeed, an Internet pay-per-view system might be one way of solving the perennial problem of liquidity that faces all opera theaters everywhere.

But there will never be a viable substitute for a seat in the theater itself. However sophisticated the technology, it can never be perfect enough to convey the hushed anticipation before a performance, or the collective thrill that an audience experiences at crucial moments.

As for what the new opera will sound like, this Cassandra sees only a clouded crystal ball. But you can safely bet on one thing: opera will be as varied and as stimulating as ever.

Divas and Divos

I hope that by now you have noticed that this is a book about operas, not singers. But I can't let you to put it down without at least some mention of these much-worshiped, and much-derided, creatures. Singers, after all, carry the weight of opera on their shoulders and have a reputation for being as dramatic offstage as on, for not being able to act and for being – shall we say – less than sylph-like in stature.

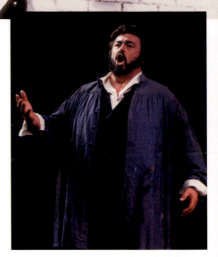

ABOVE Pavarotti in *Tosca*.

In some cases, all of these things are, or were, true. It may also be true that in these jet-setting days, the more famous the singer, the less he or she can be bothered to hang around and work at a production, as an integral part of a team. Another *Bohème?* Madame X can sing for the usual fortune, of course, but really she knows the role so well that she doesn't need to rehearse. This attitude is anathema to a successful operatic production, though it might please the thousands of canary-fanciers out there.

Fortunately, it is becoming less commonplace. Nowadays most singers – with the exception of the Pavarottis and the hyped, conspicuously dishy younger stars, like Roberto Alagna – don't demand star treatment, limousines, and the rest. They might fly Club Class for the sake of experiencing less stress (which affects both stamina and voice), but they are quite likely to arrive by metro or bus and to drift away anonymously after the performance. They are mere mortals, like the rest of us. And though, like the rest of us, they come in all shapes and sizes, this younger generation of opera singers has proved that you don't need to be of enormous proportions to sing your Wagner.

Is the fat lady singing?

Once I met a particularly slim, petite opera singer in Houston, who told me of her encounter at the immigration desk.

"What are you here for?" demanded the officer.

"I'm an opera singer, and I've come to perform at Houston Grand Opera."
[Incredulous look at this student-like waif dressed in jeans and T-shirt.]

"C'mon, lady. You don't even look like an opera singer."

"Well, if you don't believe me I'll sing."
[Suddenly alarmed.]
"Okay, go through."

MY TOP SINGERS EVER – OR TODAY, ANYWAY

Janet Baker *(b. 1933)*: Yorkshire woman who used to work in a bank, but possesses one of the most mellow mezzo-soprano sounds and an intense quality of expression that makes her perfect for music ranging from Handel to Mahler. Lacks a little power, though.

Grace Bumbry *(b.1937)*: first black singer to appear at Bayreuth (in 1961), a mezzo-soprano well able to handle Puccini's major soprano roles.

Maria Callas *(1923–77)*: drama queen *par excellence*, but a characterful, rather than pretty, voice.

Enrico Caruso *(1873–1921)*: the name everyone knows, and the first star tenor to make his name on recordings. Because of a lack of proper training, he had problems at the upper end of the register and came to rely on – and even be admired for – a sort of falsetto at that end. Convincing phrasing, though, and a wonderfully Italianate temperament, warm but explosive.

LEFT Callas as Tosca.

Fyodor Chaliapin *(1873–1938)*: Russian bass, best in Russian opera, and one of those rare creatures – a singer who could act. Another huge personality: it goes with the job. A truly international artist,

ABOVE Chaliapin as Boris Godunov.

he had an early career at the Bolshoy and Maryinsky operas, followed by appearances at La Scala, Milan, the Met, Paris, and London. He left Russia in 1921.

Placido Domingo *(b. 1934)*: A Spanish Pavarotti with the hard edges softened, and with a broader musical perspective to boot.

Voice Types

Singers – voices – fall into several different categories, but can be divided into seven groups, based on gender and range: soprano, mezzo-soprano and contralto (high, not so high, and distinctly chesty) for the women; countertenor, tenor, baritone, and bass (unnaturally high, high, low, very low) for the men. There used to be another male voice type – the castrato – but the fashion of relieving boy singers of certain aspects of their masculine potential has, mercifully, died out. I've heard of giving all for your art, but that did seem to be taking things a little too far. Anyway, within each of these categories there are other sub-categories – a tenor, for example, might be lyric or heroic. You'll find terms like *spinto* applied to soprano or tenor roles or voices. Basically, that's a lyrical sort of voice, with a lot of oomph available at passionate climaxes. *Coloratura* is another one – taken to mean a soprano (usually) who can sing a highly decorated line, with lots of fast scales and arpeggios. Easy, isn't it?

Kathleen Ferrier *(1912–53)*: died tragically young, but her very English, very round sound, a lovable personality, and a captivating stage presence endeared her to many

ABOVE Domingo in *Carmen*.

who were otherwise unacquainted with the art of singing.

Dietrich Fischer-Dieskau *(b.1925)*: versatile bass-baritone with a vast repertoire, including many of the most challenging opera scores of the century and all of Schubert's and Wolf's songs. Eyes as expressive as the voice.

Jessye Norman *(b.1934)*: criticized because of her ample proportions, but her imposing presence, which enables her to act without seeming to move, and a glorious soprano sound bring all criticism to nothing. Can be unpredictable, however.

Luciano Pavarotti *(b.1935)*: shouts, but you've got to admire the power, the chutzpah, and that formidable girth.

Elisabeth Schwarzkopf *(b.1915)*: the female Fischer-Dieskau, great at Mozart and Richard Strauss and excels in Lieder, but also, surprisingly, the first Anne Trulove in *The Rake's Progress* (see pp.108–9). Her flexible, radiant voice quality is also perfect for operetta, though sometimes she is accused of mannerism.

ABOVE Schwarzkopf in *Otello*.

Joan Sutherland *(b.1926)*: can't hear the words, but a down-to-earth Australian diva with a lovely sound and a brilliant *coloratura*.

Bryn Terfel *(b.1965)*: amiable Welsh baritone (English is his second language), who came to prominence in the early 1990s and has since risen to gigantic stature, thanks to his rounded, powerful, and flexible voice and his sometimes overwhelming stage presence. Straddles the ground between populism and high art with ease.

Willard White *(b.1946)*: a fine Porgy in Gershwin's *Porgy and Bess*, but also a towering Wotan in Wagner's *Ring*. Jamaican by birth, he has also acted as Othello.

ABOVE Terfel in *Salome*.

Of this selection, only Domingo, Norman, Pavarotti, Terfel, and White are still singing, so if someone tries to sell you a ticket for Chaliapin, he's likely to be from the local Gramophone Society.

LEFT Sutherland as Anna Bolena.

Opera Houses of the World

Australia: OPERA OF SOUTH AUSTRALIA, *Adelaide: performs in the Festival Theatre and the smaller Victorian Opera Theatre.* SYDNEY OPERA HOUSE: *built as a grand architectural gesture, but the auditorium is too small for opera.* VICTORIA STATE OPERA, *Melbourne: built as a rival to Sydney.*

Austria: STAATSOPER, *Vienna: great theater, the best casts money can buy and the snootiest audiences.* VOLKSOPER, *Vienna: devoted to the lighter side of the operatic scale.*

Belgium: OPÉRA NATIONAL DE BELGIQUE (THÉÂTRE LA MONNAIE): *Radical, stimulating productions.*

Czech Republic: NATIONAL THEATER, TYL THEATER, SMETANA THEATER, *Prague: all upholding Prague's fine operatic traditions.*

Denmark: ROYAL THEATER, *Copenhagen: a thriving company.*

Finland: HELSINKI: *most productions sung in Finnish, so brush up on the language or plot.*

France: BASTILLE OPERA, *Paris: a bit too concrete-y for some; liked for its radicalism by others.* OPÉRA COMIQUE, *Paris: part and parcel of the Paris Opéra.* PALAIS GARNIER, *Paris: the older opera house, but still in use.*

Germany: DEUTSCHE OPER, *Berlin: good record for interesting repertoire.* DEUTSCHE STAATSOPER, *Berlin.* KOMISCHE OPER, *Berlin.* WAGNER FESTSPIELHAUS, *Bayreuth: a mecca for Wagner.*

Hungary: HUNGARIAN STATE THEATER, *and the smaller* ERKEL THEATER, *Budapest: homes for a historic national company.*

ABOVE Opera buffs wait in line outside New York's Met in 1949.

Italy: LA SCALA, *Milan: dress well and expect a noisy audience.* SAN CARLOS, *Naples: ditto, only more southern and conservative.*

Netherlands: TOWN HALL MUSIC THEATER, *Amsterdam: much new and neglected work.*

Russia: BOLSHOY THEATER, *Moscow: fine native opera.* KIROV OPERA HOUSE, *St Petersburg: ditto.*

South America: TEATRO AMAZONAS, *Mánaus: Strictly one for the tourists.* TEATRO COLON, *Buenos Aires: vast, spectacular, but crumbling.* TEATRO MUNICIPAL, *Rio de Janeiro: concerts only, but a fine building.*

Spain: GRAN TEATRO DEL LICEU, *Barcelona: an excellent tradition.* TEATRO LIRICO NACIONAL DE ZARZUELA, *Madrid: not really off the ground yet in artistic terms.*

Sweden: DROTTNINGHOLM: *The authentic experience.*

Switzerland: GRAN THÉÂTRE DE GENÈVE: *rich and productive.* ZURICH STADTTHEATER: *fine early opera, plus Wagner, Verdi, etc.*

UK: THE COLISEUM, *London: crumbling, cramped opera performances, but much beloved.* GLYNDEBOURNE, *Sussex: fine new theater in the countryside.* ROYAL OPERA HOUSE, *London: currently being rebuilt. Has an enduring air of snootiness.*

U.S.A.: CHICAGO LYRIC OPERA: *high prices, largely Italian repertoire; also known for Wagner.* HOUSTON: *claims to radicalism; stages many premieres of new works.* NEW YORK CITY OPERA: *plays a more radical repertoire than the Met.* NEW YORK METROPOLITAN OPERA: *opened 1966, privately funded and thus largely conservative.* SAN FRANCISCO OPERA: *renowned for its star-studded productions.* SANTA FE OPERA: *rivals Houston as the most enterprising U.S. house.*

How to Comport Yourself in the Opera House

In the auditorium, open your ears and mind, as well as your heart. Focus on the sounds – the orchestra as well as the singers – and the sights, and ignore (if you can) the distractions of the lady rustling her jewels behind you, or the coughs of those who would much rather be at home watching opera of a more sudsy type on the TV.

That's another thing: opera-going is to some extent a social occasion. But if you feel that you're surrounded by people who dress more expensively than you and mouth off extravagantly about the time they heard Callas singing the Mad Scene in '56 or whenever – in other words, if you feel out of place – remember this: the *experience* of opera is the thing. It's okay to wear nice clothes if you want to, but not simply to score points or because it seems "proper." If you're feeling particularly rebellious, resolve to go next time wearing patched Levis and a T-shirt with something obscene inscribed upon it, and demand a beer at the bar (bearing in mind, for comfort's sake, the length of the next act!). Opera snobbery, unfortunately, is still rife, but in certain places it's slowly improving and efforts are slowly being made to Attract Ordinary Mortals With Average Incomes.

On that subject, without going mad, pay as much as you can reasonably afford for a seat. It's no good having to crane your neck from behind a pillar, only to discover that you need a pair of binoculars even to make out that huge pyramid in *Aida*. And if you have the choice of paying for a modest seat to hear a mega-star tenor singing one of the best-loved roles in all opera, or paying the same amount for a top seat at an opera that you know will be particularly interesting, then forget the star. He probably won't be able to act, anyway. Diva-worshipping has nothing to do with opera-loving – though record companies, eager to promote their product, would have us believe quite differently.

RIGHT Jessye Norman; when she sings Ariadne, you listen.

OPERA SPEAK
This selection explain terms that crop up in the text.

Aria Italian for "air" – the songs in opera that may, or may, not be self-contained "numbers."

Ariette French for "little air." Ditto the above, but slighter and lighter in flavor.

Basso profundo A deep and resonant bass voice.

Cadenza The part of an aria when the singer gives an improvisatory, highly embellished passage, often suspending a regular beat, to prove the brilliance of his or her vocal technique. Singers have been known to exceed the bounds of taste and proportion in such passages. Also a similar passage in concertos for solo instruments and orchestra.

Castrato An adult male singer who in boyhood possessed a voice of such quality that he was forcibly deprived of certain elements of his manhood-to-be. This preserved the range of his voice, while allowing it to develop. Castrati reached the height of popularity in the first half of the eighteenth century, being renowned for their skill and their sound – nasty business, really.

Chromatic The term applied to music colored by notes that aren't part of the scale of the prevailing key. In C major, that means all the sharps and flats (the black keys on the piano).

Comédie-ballet A unification of stage play and ballet. *Opéra-ballet*, a later genre, reduced dramatic content to a minimum in favor of dancing.

Continuo group The musicians (comparatively few in number) who provide the bass line and – in the case of plucked strings, harpsichord, or organ – fill in the harmonies under the vocal line.

***Da capo* aria** An aria in three sections, of which the last is a repeat – altered or not – of the first. Literally, "from the top." The instruction *Da capo al fine* (from the *beginning* to the word *fine*) appears at the end of section B, to save the writing or printing of the same music twice – the word *fine* marking the end of section A.

Dramma per musica Italian for "play for music" – the seventeenth- and eighteenth-century term for a libretto destined for music; hence, serious opera.

Ground bass aria An aria whose bass line is a short, but literally repeated, sequence of notes.

Leitmotiv A musical idea – it could be a melody, a chordal sequence, a rhythm, or even an instrumental color – that signifies an event, a feeling, a connection in a drama. Useful if you can't hear or understand the words.

Musical realism You tell me!

Opera buffa Funny opera, using characters drawn from everyday life.

Opéra comique A French operatic form, which began life as farce and satire, but developed into something more serious in the early nineteenth century.

Opera semiseria *Opera seria* that includes comic elements.

Opera seria Serious opera (very formal and complex), usually about mythological subjects, and the chief genre of the eighteenth century.

Oratorio Not opera at all, but a composition usually based on a biblical story, with dramatic and contemplative elements, and not intended to be staged.

Recitative Music intended to be sung as if it were speech (i.e., in a freely expressive rhythm).

Répétiteur The pianist who teaches the singer the notes, and often a lot about the part, well out of sight of the public.

Secco Italian for "dry" – a type of recitative used in *opera buffa* that goes very quickly and is accompanied only by the occasional stabbing chord.

Serialism Music in which the old hierarchies of key systems – with different notes of the scale having different degrees of importance – are replaced with a new system in which all 12 notes of the chromatic scale are rotated regularly in a series, melodically or harmonically (and usually both). Invented, or evolved (as he would claim), by Arnold Schoenberg, and cultivated with a softer Romantic touch by Alban Berg.

Singspiel Literally "song-play" – a German operatic form, in German, with spoken material in place of recitative.

Song-cycle A cycle of songs intended to be performed in sequence, sung from the point of view of a single character.

Structuralism The philosophical movement that views all human social phenomena – music included – in terms of wholes, rather than constituents. Broadly speaking, nothing in one constituent of a structure can be changed without affecting every other part of the structure. Got it?

Tonal The term applied to music unequivocally in a major or minor key.

Tragédie lyrique A term that was invented by Quinault and Lully and first applied to their *Cadmus et Hermione* in 1673, signifying epic or mythological subjects that are treated ostensibly in a clear and natural manner, but quickly criticized for exaggeration.

Verismo Italian for "realism" – a term applied to operas by Mascagni, Leoncavallo, and others that treat generally low-life subjects in a larger-than-life way.

Index

PHOTOGRAPHIC CREDITS

Archiv für Kunst und Geschichte,London:
18/19 (State Hermitage, St Petersburg), 28T,
30T, 31 (O. Anthrather), 32, 34/35 (Erich
Lessing/Kunsthistorische Museum, Vienna),
47 (Erich Lessing/Historisches Museum der
Stadt, Vienna), 48B, 50/51, 55T (Erich
Lessing/The Louvre), 57, 60, 68B, 92T, 93,
106T, 110 (Lotte Jocobi), 118, 122.
Catherine Ashmore: 9, 104, 105, 126.
The Bridgeman Art Library:
10 (Stapleton Coll), 12/13 (Johnny Van
Haeften Gallery), 15 (Castle Museum and Art
Gallery, Nottingham), 17T (Rafael Valls
Gallery), 22T, 23 (Earl of Pembroke), 24, 27,
34T (Kunsthistorisches Museum, Vienna),
39T, 41 and 43 (Deutsche Theater Museum,
Munich), 56M (Victoria and Albert Museum),
62 (Bristol Museum and Art Gallery), 66M
(Bibliothèque de l'Opéra), 77 (The Wagner
Museum), 82/83 (Novosti), 87B, 88
(Tretyakov Gallery, Moscow), 96 (Schoenberg
Museum, Vienna), 102 (Bibliothèque de
l'Opéra), 108 (Sir John Soane Museum),
123 (Musée des Beaux Arts, Rouen),
124B (Tretyakov Gallery, Moscow),
128 (Haags Gementemuseum), 137T
(State Russian Museum, St Petersburg).

**Giraudon/The Bridgeman
Art Library:**
21 (Musée Condé, Chantilly), 28/29 and 33
(The Louvre), 54 (Museum des Beaux Arts, Le
Havre).
**Lauros-Giraudon/The Bridgeman
Art Library:**
37 (Château de Versailles), 53B (The Louvre).
Corbis/Bettman: 35B, 139.
Zoe Dominic: 121B.
e.t. archive: 22B, 38/39, 56BL, 61, 63, 65,
70/71, 75, 78B, 79T, 85B, 90, 95, 98B, 101,
120/121, 129.
The Performing Arts Library:
Clive Barda/PAL: 11R and 55B, 116/117, 119,
130, 133, 134/135; Ron Scherl/PAL, 64/65.
Reg Wilson:
8, 11B, 14B, 16B, 20B, 40B, 44/45, 59, 67B,
69R, 73, 79B, 89T, 89B, 94, 96, 99, 101, 103,
106B, 107, 109, 111, 112, 113, 114, 115,
124/125, 127, 131, 136, 137B, 138 all, 140B.